Let Me Remember This

A Seeker's Observations and Thoughts on the Path to Understanding

---

Memory fades over time like a photograph
left in a window that catches the light.
Most of what is missing doesn't matter.
But let me remember this.

SURENDRA JAMES CONTI

DORRANCE
PUBLISHING CO
EST. 1920
PITTSBURGH, PENNSYLVANIA 15238

Dorrance Publishing Co
585 Alpha Drive
Suite 103
Pittsburgh, PA 15238
Visit our website at www.dorrancebookstore.com

ISBN: 978-1-4809-5603-2
eISBN: 978-1-4809-5580-6

Let Me Remember This

A Seeker's Observations and Thoughts
on the Path to Understanding

"Reading *Let Me Remember This* is like having a conversation with a close, trusted friend. As a writer myself, I recognize a kindred spirit in Surendra who loves the beauty of words and the subtlety they can convey. As a seeker of truth, I see through his writings a soul who is on the same quest for the meaning behind life's experiences. And as someone who has met truly wise people in my life, I acknowledge the deep wisdom he has gained. Poet, seeker, sage: Surendra is all of these, and his book is a gift to cherish for years to come."

—Nayaswami Devi, author, lecturer, and Spiritual Co-Director of Ananda Sangha Worldwide

"*Let Me Remember This* is a gem of a book that scintillates with warmth and wisdom. Gleaned from decades on the spiritual path, Surendra offers reflections, philosophical musings, life stories, dreams and insights to amuse, edify, and awaken us. His keen awareness, depth of heart and twinkle of humor make for thoroughly enjoyable reading while imparting important life lessons. *Let Me Remember This* will be a warmly welcomed companion to any seeker's library."

—Dana Lynne Andersen, Founder and Director, Awakening Arts Academy

"Surendra James Conti's book, *Let Me Remember This*, is filled with inspiration and insights, garnered from many years of introspection while following the spiritual path laid out by Paramhansa Yogananda, the great Indian master and author of the classic *Autobiography of a Yogi*. Walk along with him as he takes you on a delightful journey from one beautiful thought-vista to the next, each insight directed toward the highest goal of Self-realization."

—Richard Dayanand Salva, author, *The Yoga of Abraham Lincoln* and numerous other books

"Reading Surendra's *Let Me Remember This* feels like engaging in an inspiring and captivating conversation with a close friend in my own living room... like he's holding up a mirror for me to see and experience my true, higher self in a number of different ways. Highly recommended reading."

—Bill Grady, author, *Beacons of Light*

"In this beautifully written book, Surendra shares his journey, filled with very human experiences, insights, struggles, and devotion to the guidance of his beloved guru, Paramhansa Yogananda, and that of his spiritual teacher Swami Kriyananda. These pages are of his quest to move beyond egoic consciousness and remember the bliss and depth of the True Self. May we all, with the support of whatever path or wisdom tradition we follow, remember this."

—Manohar Croke, author, *Energy Psychology Using Light and Color*

"Reading this book is like having an interesting conversation with a wise friend. Surendra has the gift of putting into words, the questions, and many of the answers, that intrigue all sincere truth seekers. Open the book anywhere. It will lighten your heart and give you something interesting to think about for the rest of the day. Highly recommended."

—Asha Praver, author, *Ask Asha, Loved and Protected* and *Swami Kriyananda: As We Have Known Him*

Dedication

To the loves of my life, who are many, but especially to Mom, who believed in me even when I doubted myself; to Tushti, my wife, who was at my side and often a little ahead for thirty-five wonderful years; to the Muse, who inspires me more than she knows; to my beloved guru, Paramhansa Yogananda, the saint I never knew in this life but likely have known for ages; and to Swami Kriyananda, who taught me the purpose of life by living it every minute.

———————

I also wish to give special thanks to graphic artist David Jensen for his inspiring cover and interior design.

Preface

My life has not been one of extremes, nor of exceptional drama. But in the course of my years, I have seen changes in the world that have far exceeded the science fiction of my youth. The age of atomic energy, which exploded into existence when I was a child of two, has since given way to a dozen successors, the latest of which is the age of virtual reality. What next? We have landed men on the moon, mapped and demystified the wonders of the human brain; and now, in our startling output of innovation, it seems we have come to the brink of wonder's demise. Who is surprised by anything anymore?

I have been journaling my thoughts and observations since the 1970s. This book is one of selections I have culled from that volume of work, ranging widely in content, with an emphasis on my inward journey. *Let Me Remember This*, the title I have chosen, is intended to be a reminder to me to live the teachings that I have been blessed to receive and put into words.

This book is not meant to be read from cover to cover. A chapter or an essay a day will hopefully offer enough for you to think about before reading on. Opening at random to any page may also prove useful. Often with books of this kind, I find that I have been guided to a piece that I especially needed to consider at that particular time.

You will find some repeated themes, images and examples throughout the book. That is because the path to higher awareness is simpler—although not easier to travel—than we tend to suppose. A certain amount of repetition, as a means of reinforcing what is essential, becomes an important part of the guidance that is given.

The thoughts that are recorded here are a compilation of what I have learned from over seventy years of living, and especially from others. The words are mine, and the thoughts themselves are mine now as well, but in sharing them, I am merely astride the shoulders of many wiser teachers and great souls before me. My gratitude has no end.

Contents

Dedication   v

Preface   vii

Introduction   15

Chapter 1: Dreamers and the Dream   21
  Dreamers and the Dream
  The Incredible Me
  Row, Row, Row Your Boat

Chapter 2: Desire   31
  All We Want
  A few more reflections

Chapter 3: Reason and Reality   37
  From Mansion to Cell
  Really, Maybe, Not
  How Reasonable Is Reason?
  Form, Function and Freud
  Be Thou a Yogi
  Essay-ettes

Chapter 4: Truth   55
  And the Truth Shall Set You Free
  On the Trail of Truth and Treasure

Chapter 5: Faith   65

Such As We Are

You Have God Already

Finding Happier

Is God the Source of Evil Too?

In Pursuit of Devotion

Who Is a True Christian?

Chapter 6: The Quest   85

Reeling on the Road to Redemption

I and Other

Held by the Holding

Imagine the Possibilities

Chapter 7: Love   95

Love Is a Kind of Literacy

Start Where You Are

Love at First Sight

In the Sway of Peril's Way

Essay-ettes

Chapter 8: Death and Dying   105

What Comes Around

Like a River in the Desert of Time

In Search of Transcendence

Essay-ette

Willingness and Faith

Essay-ette

Chapter 9: Mind Games   123

The Tree and the Angel

Thinking Out of the Box

Blinded by the Mind

Chapter 10: Into the Great Within   133

Dare to Be Different

Welcome to the Monkey House

Working through the Wobblies

Chapter 11: Rants and Remedies   143

Poem: Treebone Parks
We Are One Who See Two
Almost a Poem, Ever a Plea
Poem: A Short History of the U.S. in Vietnam
Dealing with Trouble
Essay-ettes / Food for Thought

Chapter 12: Almost Everything Else   155

Essay-ettes
Hey, Just Get Over It!
Noble Is as Noble Does
Courage of Many Kinds
Remember to Self-Forget
It's Complicated. Or Isn't It?
The Rise of Informania

Chapter 13: Poetry   175

Leaving the Loop
I Come to the Sea
Less and Less / Paradox
A Song for the Road
The Difference
In Flint Is the Fire
Into the Deep / I Could Not See What I Could Be
Distraction
The Way It Seems to Be
Deadlines
To the Guru
December
Slipping Away / When?
Archer, Seek the Shaft of Light
Get Along, Little Self, Get Alone

Chapter 14: On Writing   193

Essay-ettes: The Way We Are

Chapter 15: Essays in a Sentence or Two   199

Chapter 16: A Few More Personals: Then and Now   207

Introduction

G reetings and welcome. . .

As an avid observer of people and their ways, and as a lover of life in all of its familiar, peculiar and inscrutable manifestations, I invite you to join me here on a journey into the wilds of what I have seen. To a great extent my experience, though unique, is collectively ours. We have both been alive for many years, sharing our hopes and fears, victories and frustrations, joys and woes.

For this reason and more, I hope you will find these pages engaging, provocative and worthwhile. But first, if you wish, here's a bit about me.

I was born in 1943 in Texas, where I lived for all of six weeks. My father, a medical doctor, was briefly stationed in the Army at Fort Hood in Waco, and that's when I appeared on the scene. When he shipped out to the Philippines during World War II, I lived with my mother and grandparents in Chicago until he returned.

In 1947 our family, which now included the first of my two sisters, migrated west to Southern California, where Dad opened his medical practice with another radiologist he had met overseas. Those were the heady years of post-war renewal, a great time to be kid.

In the late '40s and early '50s, America was in its prime and on the move. Occasional mushroom clouds over barren Nevada deserts testified to a new kind of war that loomed in potential, but an optimistic mood prevailed across the land. I see that period now as a montage of scrapbook images set to Paul Simon's tender elegy *Old Friends*. . .

"Time it was, and what a time it was,

A time of innocence, a time of confidences,

Long ago it must be, I have a photograph. . ."

Admittedly what I remember of my first 20 years is overridingly pleasant, and maybe that's one of the beauties of getting older. Even our painful memories are softened and sometimes reconfigured with touches of sweetness and humor. It wasn't until November 22, 1963, that the world changed for me and my generation. It happened in barely an instant. The assassination of President John Kennedy took the innocence out of our sails.

The journey that has led me here has meandered through many careers and occupations. Writing, though I've always enjoyed it, had to wait for my earlier dreams to cool and die in the face of absurdly steep opposing odds: dreams that included being a rodeo cowboy; spearing line drives for the LA Dodgers; saving lives as a celebrated surgeon, and arguing legal cases before the Supreme Court. Still, my life has been richly served in ways I never imagined could or would be.

As a youth, I delivered newspapers on a bike that had one gear, and I caddied at a country club when golfers actually walked a course on foot. On summer breaks from college I wrangled horses at a ranch camp in Carmel Valley, labored as a "roustabout" in dusty Los Angeles oil fields, and worked on an assembly line in a fruit-drink bottling plant. That last job paid a whopping $3.12 an hour.

In 1965, in the months between graduation and a one-year stretch in law school, I sold food-stocked freezers door-to-door in Watts until the city was torched in the August riots that redefined civil disobedience in California.

For a few months I drove a truck for UPS, then landed a trainee position at a marquee LA advertising agency. Three years later I was part of the Magic Kingdom, writing the ads for Disneyland, and producing its radio and TV :30s and :60s. On the strength of that credential, I launched into 18 years of freelance commercial work for various agencies, dba Conti Creative. I lived mostly then in Honolulu, where I met and married my wife Patti, an RN at Kaiser Hospital, and where I also later became an art dealer, specializing in original Old Master prints.

Our careers were interrupted in 1990 by a windfall profit from the sale our condominium, which we turned into ten glorious months of around-the-world travel. Riding the crest of that wave, we moved to Seattle, and soon thereafter were headed for its trough. Life changes quickly when get-rich ideas cause a loss of perspective. It was there that I drove us into debt with a network-marketing plan to amass a fortune. This was not only humbling, it required that I find high-paid work in a field I never would have entered otherwise; I hit the road as a salesman on straight commission for a number of years, placing a variety of products in retail stores and restaurants. Thankfully, I was good at closing deals, and we recovered nicely.

During this time we began to explore the deeper world within ourselves, and were drawn to the weekend workshops and channeled presence of the spirit-warrior Ramtha in Yelm, Washington. It was not until 1996, however, that our inner lives changed significantly. My wife (who was later given the spiritual name Tushti, meaning contentment) coaxed me to join her in a meditation class at a place called Ananda. This set us both firmly on a spiritual path that has, above all, revealed to me who I am, why I am here, and what this human jitterbug is all about.

I have since added more careers to my eclectic resume. In 2002, at Ananda's request, we moved to its Palo Alto community to manage its flagship East West Bookshop, where we served for over nine years. Renowned as a resource for higher awareness, the store is the largest of its genre in America, dedicated to the New Consciousness movement, and offering a vast array of products and programs that complement its mission.

A second Ananda career, which probably does not include any other former food-stocked freezer salesmen, has been that of a spiritual minister, known as a Lightbearer. Tushti and I were ordained in 2007. The only downside to this great honor and blessing is a duty to walk the high road when temperament and temptation would prefer a timeout. It reminds me of what Saint Augustine said in a rare moment of weakness: "Lord, help me to be good, but not yet!"

In 2012 we shifted again, this time to India, to serve Ananda's mission of bringing the teachings of our guru, Paramhansa Yogananda, to the land of his birth. This assignment continued until late 2015, when Tushti was diagnosed with pancreatic cancer, and we returned to American soil, where she bravely and peacefully passed away a few months later. She was my best friend for 35 years, and I miss her a lot.

I make my home near Portland, Oregon now, where I manage Ananda's Portland Temple and Teaching Center, and where I continue to write in much the same vein as you will find reflected on the pages that follow.

In this book's essays and commentaries, you will meet my heroes, encounter my peeves, hopefully enjoy the humor that underlies most of our fears and frustrations, and hopefully too, find a wealth of ideas that could be applied to make this world a happier, healthier place for all who share it.

Joy to you. . .

Surendra

CHAPTER I

Dreamers and the Dream

We search. We explore. We discover. In the end we find we are back where our search began, seeing at last that all is a dream, that all is God, that our quest was only to know who we are and rise to the occasion.

DREAMERS AND THE DREAM

What is life? What is it for? What is the point of it anyway?

The short answer, I suppose, is that none of us really knows. We're here for a while and then we're not. Some things seem to make sense, others don't. It's like a colossal mystery sprinkled with occasional clues. God only knows the why of it all. But like everyone else, I have my own ideas. Here they are. . . .

Life is a dream. Its reality is a reverie that veils a deeper truth. Nothing about it endures.

Somewhere unseen is the Dreamer of what we are and what we see. He isn't a he, and yet He is the source, the life, and the single true reality of all that is. He is everywhere, in everything, and in us. To those with a mind to notice, He appears wherever we look, although we mostly overlook that He's there, thinking we have more important things to identify and address.

Within the Dreamer's dream, we are dreamers too. We have dreams of self-concern that occupy our waking and sleeping hours. They are little dreams, like drops in the sea, most of them egoic and rather silly. Many little dreamers also dream that life has no meaning or logic. This is a very bad dream, maybe the silliest of all.

In the Dreamer's dream, we have the power to think and do as we choose. We can fill each moment of life with love. Or with something else. Many choose something else most of the time, and all of us do now and then. That's what causes our little dreams to turn us upside down.

In our little dreams, we are often quite inventive. We imagine, for example, that matter matters a lot. And many imagine that what matters most is how much matter you have.

In the Dreamer's dream, life has a greater purpose. Patiently and lovingly, He is waiting for us to get it. He is waiting for us to choose to make it our own. He apparently has an exceptional sense of humor. And no real sense of time.

The Dreamer's dream has two features that tend to give us fits: duality and physical death. You would think we would have adjusted to this by now, but for some inexplicable reason, most of us spend our days trying to deny or outwit them. In our little dreams the goodies we get are gotten free and clear of hitches and glitches. We dream that satisfaction will endure. It's a laughable idea that fails to make us laugh.

From time to time the Dreamer sends extra help, hoping to straighten us out. Enlightened ones appear, offering guidance to where duality and death have been dreamt away. A few little dreamers take heed. Turning inward, we begin to see the light of a new understanding, of who and what we truly are, of what this dream of life is all about. We discover that matter, in mattering less, leads to peace of mind. We experience a swelling of love and joy. In waking to the Dreamer instead of the dream, we find ourselves finally headed for happily ever after.

THE INCREDIBLE ME

Nothing amazes me more than the realization of who I am.

I don't mean "me" as a set of self-definitions; I mean that now and forever, this being in the body that I presently carry around, is someone that only I can be. There is no option here. I cannot trade my consciousness, my karma, or my future with anyone else. I am who I am for the whole of eternity's ever and a day. When I think about that, especially when my deficiencies are on display, it's rather disconcerting.

Are you ever struck by that awareness too? You are you, a consciousness for all perpetuity, and there's nothing you can do about that except to carry on.

I suppose there is some consolation in seeing that we are *like* everyone else. But in likeness is where the resemblance ends. No one else can know what it is to be me, nor am I always sure of this myself.

Eastern sages tell us that all of this world is a dream. Yet, the dreamy point of view that you and I possess. . . well, it just isn't the same. We interpret according to our own specific desires and predispositions, many of which have doubtless been hauled forward from past incarnations. Each of us may be inching toward a consciousness of unity, but our progress continues to suffer the millennial delays of our delusions. Here, again, though we tend to self-obstruct in similar ways, I have my own unique manners and methods, and so do you.

Within this universal dream, human nature is, for me, its most fascinating feature. I love how people get so wrapped up in their personal notions of what is what, and what each what implies! Rarely do we pause to consider, as my guru affirmed, that "Circumstances are always neutral." It is only our reaction to them that gives them a particular charge. And this, of course, is what causes us to careen out of control, into labyrinths of unpaved, hard-scrabble karma.

Few lessons are as hard to grasp as this one: that how we see the world and its goings-on says nothing about *them* and everything about *us*. Society has thrown its full weight behind the idea that circumstances are either pro or con, and it has trained us to judge whatever we perceive, to develop likes and dislikes, and to seek satisfaction in pursuit of material and egoic fulfillment. But in truth it is these reactive conclusions that condemn us to every suffering we accept.

As long as we adhere to society's pro-or-con criteria, we are bound to wind up worshipping our mistakes. Only at the quiet center of perception, in the stillness that is the altar of God, does suffering disappear. There alone, in the moment, is where worldly desires and attachments are given no time to establish roots, and where freedom awaits.

Okay, so you're not there yet, and neither am I. This is the downside of coming to grips with being the one and only you that is you. By degrees, though, we are all in route to the same blissful summit. Our mission is simply to keep climbing, calmly active and actively calm, with the aim of owning our delusions and desires along the way.

For seventeen years, in observing the life of Swami Kriyananda, I was blessed to take note of what that calmness becomes. He lived as one whose knowledge of God emanates from direct experience. No parallel to this can be found in mental genius. It dwarfs the counsel of the keenest and most powerful intellect. And above all, it inspires. I could see in his life's journey the potential that all of us have, the ability to break through the clouds that hover above us. I could see that the difference between us was merely in what we had managed to surrender. He was at ease with God alone, and I was—and am—still held by thoughts and things which I imagine to be mine. I could see in him how a saint is forged.

Kriyananda's guru, Paramhansa Yogananda, taught him to reside in the center of his being, where there is "center everywhere, circumference nowhere." All true religions uphold essentially the same ideal. It is only their phrasing of it that is apt to vary. Becoming "center everywhere" is the goal that Jesus emphasized throughout his ministry, the goal that gives to all of us "the power to become the Sons of God."

When I arrived at the trailhead of my own spiritual path, I, like most, was packing a hefty load of conventional luggage: namely, a sense of God as external to me, a heavily IQ-based education, and a steady diet of Darwinian competitiveness in all matters ranging from love to war. In short, my ego was a fixture at the helm of who I had become. Even today it remains a tenacious, though seemingly well intentioned foe. My ego and I have quarreled over every soul-supportive step I have taken. And many have not been taken yet because of its forceful nature.

In finally turning toward God, I would underscore two observations about my journey. First, its effect on me has been subtle, not dramatic. I have no sudden, life-changing episodes to report. Nothing akin to St. Paul's blinding conversion on the road to Damascus. But second, the accumulation of subtle effects can become dramatic over time. I can tell you that spiritual progress, like progress on any other path, is most of all a function of showing up to give it a go. One day at a time. Striving always, as Ram Dass encourages, to "Be here now."

Although we cannot inhabit each other's mind, at least not precisely, and although we are ultimately in this dream alone, the lessons we have to learn are entirely the same. After all, we are cut of the same cloth. Our destiny is One. How we differ depends on how much "circumference" we still entertain. In the end, which Yogananda described as endlessness, our ties to this contentious adventure will dissolve, and we will discover that we are *more* than we ever imagined. With courage and good cheer, let us carry on.

ROW, ROW, ROW YOUR BOAT

You've probably heard it said that time is just an illusion. Space too. Einstein essentially proved the point over a hundred years ago. But can you envision this world, or even the world of your own experience, without time and space to maintain order as we know it, to keep things from smooshing into a blobby mass of utter confusion? I can't. I don't think the human mind is capable of such a perception.

I know that in walking, driving, or flying from Portland to San Francisco, it is going to take me a certain length of time, because there's a lot of space I will need to cover. Yet, we read that many saints and ascended masters, in particular those mentioned in *Autobiography of a Yogi*, are able to be in two places at once! At some level of consciousness, time and space apparently pose no barrier to such amazing feats of mobility.

Even science has verified by experimentation that space and time are ultimately unreal. At the speed of light, they get so compressed, they lose whatever it is that distinguishes them from each other. Incredible!

Okay, so maybe we have to accept the math, but who can see in his mind an image of past and future collapsing into Now and Now Alone? No more separation, no more in between. I still don't get it.

Yet, I have to admit, it is easy to see how space has been dramatically cut down in size, and there is less of it every year to restrict our goings on and goings about. News from around the world comes to us almost instantly through satellite communication. We no longer wait for letters to arrive; we have text messaging, email, Skype, Facebook and other social media to eliminate our sense of distances. Air travel to faraway places that once took months to reach takes only a matter of hours. Space just ain't what it used to be!

This is heady stuff, but in fact a sweet old song can help us make better sense of it.

One of the oldest pieces of American music, which is still sung today, is a simple little ditty that every American child learns. It is actually a nursery rhyme that was written in the early 1850s, and was later put to music: *Row, Row, Row*

Your Boat. If you grew up in the USA, it is one of those songs you never forget, even if not having sung it for fifty years. It has only four short lines, mainly done as a sing-a-long and performed as a round in sections.

> Row, row, row your boat,
> Gently down the stream,
> Merrily, merrily, merrily, merrily,
> Life is but a dream.

You're probably singing it to yourself right now. The melody and lyrics are light and cheerful, seemingly of no significance except for the smiles they tend to invite. But I wonder if you—or any of the millions who sing this song every year in schools, at picnics, and at happy family gatherings—have tuned into the very profound message that is being conveyed. There is not a wasted word in the whole eighteen of them in this composition. Even those that repeat, repeat for a reason.

"Row, row, row your boat." In other words, give yourself energetically to your duties, your work, your relationships and responsibilities, and especially to your spiritual practices. Each of us has a distance to go, and unless we make the effort in the right direction, the boat that is our divine potential cannot arrive at where we want to be. Rowing your boat is about devoting yourself to your life's high purpose.

"Gently down the stream." But row relaxed. Enjoy the experience. Seek to steer your course in such a way as to stay in the natural flow of it. Be sensitive and at ease, never tense or resistant.

"Merrily, merrily, merrily, merrily." The repetition of this one word is intended to drive it deep into the singer's subconscious mind. We're affirming a positive outlook, prompting ourselves to look for the opportunity and joy in whatever comes before us. Happiness is a choice, and you can choose it even in the most difficult situations. Be merry, and you will be traveling downstream with a lighter stroke instead of rowing against it in a sweat.

"Life is but a dream." Now there's the real kicker! Have you heard that somewhere before? One of Ananda's theme songs is entitled *Life Is a Dream*, its wise and poignant phrases set to a beautiful melody. This is not merely a philosophical statement, it is a reminder that nothing of a sensory nature that draws our attention, that calls to us to go ashore and seek our happiness there, is anything but a bubble that is bound to pop, leaving no trace of itself. The lure of life beyond the stream—beyond the flow of energy in the astral spine, directed to the Infinite Sea—is baited with false promises of satisfaction that are certain to disappoint.

Believe it or not, this takes us back to our discussion of time, and by association, its relation to free will and our ultimate destiny. A debate in modern science, and also in religion, is whether we are free to choose, or if everything we think we are choosing has actually been predetermined. I don't know the answer, but I do know this: It doesn't make any difference. Here's why. . . .

If we have free will, and nothing has been determined until it takes place, then we are the ones rowing the boat, and where it goes is up to us. We can row toward God or away from Him, and what happens as a result will unfold according to which direction we choose, and to how much effort we apply to the oars.

If everything has been predetermined, however, it would seem that not only do we not have free will, but also that we have no control over where the boat is going, or what we are bound to become along the way. Right? Not quite, for even if the future has already been established, we have no idea what that future is, and we are bound to find out. In other words, if life is a dream, or even if it isn't, we still have to row the boat.

All of this may sound crazy, but this is a crazy planet, and even though we're its most advanced species, we're also the one that is most prone to confusion, due mainly to our penchant for wanting to figure things out that are better left to higher attunement and intuitive guidance. Christ, Krishna, Moses, the Buddha, great gurus and sages of East and West, can untie the knots in our heads with ancient wisdom that modern science still has yet to acknowledge. Even a simple old song can unravel the gist of seemingly complex topics, setting us more quickly on the course we are meant to travel and the purpose we are meant to fulfill.

We are in this dream to merge with the Dreamer: to find God. Every other pursuit is dreamier than useful; in fact, it is pointless.

Getting to God is not a mental process. It is love that must row the boat. It is love that will take us to the open sea, to the Sea of Divine Bliss. It is love that collapses time and space, rendering them insignificant. Love God. Love one another. That's really all that we have to know and do.

CHAPTER 2

Desire

"Desire, my great enemy, with his soldiers surrounding me,
is giving me lots of trouble, o' my Lord."

The opening words of a chant by Paramhansa Yogananda

ALL WE WANT . . .
is what we want when we want it!

C'mon, is that so bad? What's wrong with wanting to get ahead? Isn't that why we're here?

The U.S. Army used to have a recruitment campaign that sent a powerful message: "Be all that you can be." The reference was to character, courage, and mental and physical fitness. It wasn't to fame, fortune, or social position. These last three are absolutely *not* why we are here. Nor is having what we want when we want it, unless that wanting is communion with God.

To serve our vainglorious wishes, it's amazing how convoluted our thinking can be. Our pursuit of worldly pleasures, aggressively promoted by our social and financial systems, has turned the ego into our arbiter of worth. The trouble is, as the ego should know by now, getting what you want means getting what comes with it—the flip side of the coin—and that is never a welcome guest in anybody's experience. Isaac Newton made this clear in his incontrovertible Third Law of Motion: for every action there is an equal and opposite reaction.

Strangely, though, this proven standard seldom seems to deter us from wanton desires. And the consequences, like clockwork, follow in tow. If we are as smart as we like to believe, why haven't we figured this out and changed our ways?

Forgive me if I turn this into a rant. I assure you my own predilections are the principal target. It's just that here we are, blessed by the presence of great saints and sages, whose lives shine through the ages like beacons of Light divine, and yet we continue to look for guidance in the lifestyle of shallow celebrities and icons of greed. If this is smart, what is stupid?

Satellite technology and laboratory discoveries are testaments to our inventive talents, but what do we really *know*? As a collective, we are clueless of how to channel our energies into peace of mind and lasting joy. We're not very good at loving our neighbors either.

But we certainly are accomplished at investing in our mortal skills and ambitions, which, along with our physical bodies, are bound to arrive at the same "dead" end. We've convinced ourselves that freedom and wealth are synonymous.

Which brings me to another question: Do we even understand what freedom is? Is it the power to get, keep, and be whatever we want when we want it? If so, then freedom is just an arrangement of seven letters to symbolize the absurd. Reality—*i.e.* the rule of duality that governs this planet—does not allow that definition to work.

True freedom, however, is not a myth. It simply requires more of us than most are willing to give. Where self-indulgent desires are at stake, sacrifice is not a test we avidly undertake. And this is peculiar too, because every known Scripture, from the Bible to the Bhagavad Gita, from the Torah to the Koran, promises everlasting bliss, peace and liberation for the mere price of putting God first.

Here's another not-so-humorous effect of our acquisitive disposition: The more we acquire in quest of freedom's mantle, the more we are the acquired. Bondage begins with having more than is needed, for the habit of it incites the need for more. This also causes a particular pattern of blindness, the primary symptom of which is failing to see the strings that thereby attach to our movable parts, turning us into habit's marionettes.

All true spirituality leads to the soul within. What it leaves behind is the seeking of self in outward activities and possessions. At Ananda, where I make my home, one of the keys to progressing inward is that of renunciation. This, for us, is not a vow of poverty, but rather a commitment to simple, modest living. I find the rewards exceptional. As I shed my acquisitive urges—not even close to all of them, for I am no model of saintly ways—I am shedding as well the pressures, expenses, and stresses that wanting needless things is sure to attract.

To understand renunciation correctly is to realize its thoroughly positive nature. "It isn't the giving up of anything except misery," declared Paramhansa Yogananda. He called letting go of worldly desires "a divine investment, by which our few cents of self-discipline will yield a million spiritual dollars."

One of these days, I swear, I am going to take that wisdom to the bank. It's as clear in my mind as can be, which makes my nagging resistance to it all the more ridiculous. My own partial experience with renunciation affirms Yogananda's statement. The more "stuff" I am able to do without, the more secure I feel. It's those "few cents of self-discipline" that are so hard to invest.

At least for now I can gradually chip away at my opposition, trying to ignore the ego's Lorelei voice in my head as it constantly pleads its case. "Listen," it says, "I am with you. I want to find God too. But hey, what's the hurry? Think about all the good times we'll miss if we start moving too fast. Look around. There's so much to go for. I know that pleasures fade, but when they do, we'll find something else to replace them. Just tell me what you want, and I'll weave the allure. God will still be there. What's the hurry?"

Pinocchio learned what the hurry is when Pleasure Island morphed into a nightmare. Allowing the ego to call the tune does more than delay our redemption. It perpetuates our experience of fear and pain. For Pinocchio this epiphany came in the cavernous belly of Monstro the whale. As one who prefers his lessons meted out in subtler fashion, I would not relish the drama of such an event. And I pray this is not what it's going to take for us, as a world, to finally become as smart as we claim to be.

———————

A few Easter week reflections....

As history confirms, the human mind is nothing if not fickle. It sways to and fro on breezes of popular opinion, seasonal fashion, romantic notion and political correctness. And so it ordains the disappointing result, assuring that it will be drawn again to the lure of delusion's den.

There can be no extreme of fickleness, nor a more painful finale, to compete with the last five days of Jesus' life. Having earlier raised Lazarus from the dead, turned water into wine, and performed countless other miraculous feats, Jesus entered Jerusalem on Passover's eve, hailed by ecstatic thousands as King of the Jews, our Savior, and the Messiah. Multitudes laid palm fronds in his path, that his feet would not deign to touch the earth. Hosannas filled the air along his entire route down the Mount of Olives and into the city.

And yet within days the cheering turned to cries for his crucifixion with no more provocation than a campaign of innuendo and lies by the Pharisees' high priesthood to portray him as a necromancer, religious pretender, and threat to Judaic laws. People's faith in Jesus evaporated as fast as a desert rain. The beloved became the condemned in a stunning turn of conspiratorial events, but in the end it was the vagrant mind, prone to fear and suggestion, mercurial in its allegiance, that put Jesus to death.

It is not a stretch, I think, to find parallels between then and now of an equally destructive nature, merely more subtle and gradual in appearance. A large part of our trouble is that people seldom make commitments today; they make "temporary alliances" instead: in business, in marriage, in society. Certainty and loyalty are no longer a match for the "relative truths," fluid ideals, and shifting sands of the age.

Personal desire is the principal driver now, much as it was in Jesus' time. Or is it fear? The two share the same coin as its opposite sides. What is it we think we can draw to ourselves by our capricious ways: anything that will give us pleasure for more than a couple of days? anything that will free us from our own misguided perceptions? Does anyone think that hard times are not what our self-serving behaviors have decreed?

There's a kind of systemic chaos that seems to have spread among us. Greed and fear have caused it, and our pharmacies cannot cure it. Commitment and loyalty to cooperative living—simple, high-minded living—is the only antibiotic that can right us and right our world from the inside out. For those of fickle mind, the next few years are likely to be real killers.

The greater part of what we do is devoted to what we hope to get. We want to get things, get love, get fun, get rest, get peace, get recognized, and get ahead of the crowd. How we proceed, of course, is the story of what we have learned or what we haven't. Some of us work, some cheat, and some do little but wish and whine. But in the end it is not the getters who get what they most desire, it is they who give. Only the givers know what it takes to be happy, because only when we give is the getting good. It is they who give who get what everyone wants.

CHAPTER 3

Reason and Reality

"When we try to pick out anything by itself,

we find it hitched to everything else in the universe."

John Muir

FROM MANSION TO CELL

God only knows what it would be like to incarnate on some other planet, in some other animate form. No doubt we would deal with challenges, misconceptions and plenty of "Oops," as we do here. Perhaps there would also be "folks" like me, who find a twisted delight in the foolishness that occurs in an imperfect world.

In praise of our human species, however, it must be said that we do exhibit many exceptional talents. We invent, produce and refine all manner of time-saving devices (which would be even more impressive if time could actually be saved). We manage to adapt to conditions that test us severely. And we excel in feats of daring, whether sensible or not.

But we also excel in misunderstanding the very nature of being.

Because we cannot "see" that physical reality is born of non-physicality, we are disinclined to believe it. What we *do* see appears to have real substance, texture and shape. It stimulates our senses. But should that excuse our extra-sensory blindness? We have before us the teachings and accounts of countless avatars and saints, each revealing an accessible state of unfading bliss that requires only a redirection of where and how we focus. Yet, we commonly dismiss them as unrelated to the practicalities of living a desirable life.

Somewhere out there—and also within us—are galaxies spun of a quantum soup that is nothing more and nothing less than divinely endowed Consciousness. Of that are all things made that our minds believe to be matter. Of that are the thoughts we think. Of that is the Source that makes us one with all that is, now and evermore.

But instead of embracing this greater reality with faith, we have narrowed our focus from mansion to cell, becoming creatures of habit and limitation. We affix ourselves to Source's material disguises, telling ourselves that to lose the highs and lows of our fixations would be to lose who we are. So deeply ingrained is this perception in our collective thinking that rare is the person who dares to break its grip. Habit is clearly a jailer that frowns on granting parole. Each of us either escapes or dies deluded in his cell.

The exchanging of delusive habits for higher awareness is, as humanity's record confirms, a multi-multi-multi-millennial process. It starts with a turn to humility, believing in that which is greater than ourselves, and it does not end until we surrender completely to the Consciousness that is our Lord-Creator-God. Those who have forged themselves in fundamentalist dogma—who use the G-word like a hammer—are still missing the fullness of God's message. He is the eternal That from which, through which, and within which all exists. Religions do not define Him—or Her or the Nameless, if you prefer—unless they embrace with loving kindness the non-exclusive aspect of His Being. Which is to say, religions do not define Him.

Life is of a center, as Paramhansa Yogananda declared—"Center everywhere, circumference nowhere"—and yet we imagine an array of alluring spokes. Fame, fortune, power, relationships, and more lead us restlessly outward, far from its calm hub, to a rim that turns and turns with us in tow. We are, to put it plainly, infatuated with spinning, and largely out of control at that.

But why? Not one who has ever communed with God has called it overrated. Each has renounced all else as meriting not a moment of one's earthly desires. And still we chase those dreams and ephemeral sensations, committed to the endless dance of duality's rhythm and blues. We cling to the fantasy that lasting happiness can be found in worldly possessions and pursuits. Desperately we ignore the ubiquitous evidence that only unending struggle must ensue from this belief. We share the persistence of miseries—here today, gone tomorrow, here again and again—while death alone erases the slate in wait of another next incarnation.

Humanity is, in the words of an old song, "looking for love in all the wrong places." Few are they who recognize the folly of their ways, and among them are vastly fewer who look within. Misunderstanding the nature of being is apparently more understandable than getting it right. We are taught throughout our lives to cultivate a personality that will guard against the blows that are meted out by the whims of fate. Our egos develop into our defenders, and in the course of this, they assume command of our thoughts, feelings, and longings, determining who we perceive ourselves to be.

The God-essence that resides in the root of our being becomes inexorably buried under the sheer weight of external preoccupation. We soon forget in the scheme of egoic distraction that matter matters not, that worldly goals are goads of little or no redeeming value. Our inner selves yield the right of way to sets of rules, codes of conduct, scripted behaviors, and cravings that paralyze our ability to comprehend more.

In short, we tend to mistake how we seem for how we truly are. And thus we disallow how we could be. Instead we apply ourselves to another diet, to a change of clothes or career, to a new style designed by people who are paid to corral and brand us. We trust to the "expertise" of those who have not a clue what we need, and then we wonder why our needs persist and even deepen. The pursuit of image outstrips our investment in the greater meaning of self. And our investment in communing with God, our greater Self, is left to languish. The ego sees it only as a competition it cannot abide.

In a sense we pretend to be less than we are. Failing to grasp our full potential, we obstruct the flow of gifts and grace which the universe otherwise offers. And so it is, for ourselves and those who follow, that we continue to misunderstand the nature of being.

Really, Maybe, Not

We see, and we believe. Isn't that right? We see a chair. It's right over there. Yup, that's a chair, all right. We can see it and sit in it too. But is that enough to say that its physical reality is real?

Real or not, it would be extremely unwise to ignore the possibility that chairs and other perceived objects exist. An oncoming train will quickly dispatch both you and your quantum theory if you choose to stand in its way, expecting its atomic particles to suddenly behave as waves. Better to believe that a train is a real train.

But there is a greater reality than what our senses can experience, and failing to adhere to it causes problems that nag and never quit. This greater reality is the spectrum of the soul. Strangely, though, most of us give it little consideration. Because it does not conform to any method that science can measure, we hesitate to trust it. Hence the fix we are in.

The material world cannot be denied. As we are to live on earth, the material world is where that living must be. But here's the rub: To abide in material consciousness, as society has trained us to do, is to fear an end to what it can offer, and end it will. Moreover, this state of mind kindles material desires, which flare into attachments, which spur the creation of possessive habits, which encourage more of the same until we are fully ensnared in suffering's web. What a choice to make! But who of us, more or less, has not made it?

A question I still have to ask myself is why I would be afraid to die. The answer, always the same, stares me right in the face. Like Karna in the Bhagavad Gita, part of me wants to believe that real happiness can somehow be won on this finite plane of existence, and it urges me to give chase. This, I am constantly reminded, is absurd. The finite, after all, cannot yield an infinite result. Yet, though I am well aware that physical death is a natural aspect of life—that the real "*I*" inside my borrowed body will go on—my mortal side continues to want the cake and eat it too.

One of the lessons of the Bhagavad Gita is that none of us shrinks, but rather expands, in ousting the ego-born aspects of our personalities. Ingrained as they may seem to be, they are merely expressions of energy which, when directed inward and upward instead of outward, diminish suffering and add to our joy. The self is not lost, it is lifted.

Likewise, it should motivate us that life on earth is but a series of lessons that lead us higher to the promise of infinitely more. We cannot die except to the millions of wishes that stand in our way. It is crazy to hold fast to their fleeting amusements, to endure with disappointment their limitations. And yet that is what we incline to do, ready to excuse with reason the reason why.

Wrestling with restless thoughts goes on. But as every saint and avatar has assured us, a willingness to engage more deeply, to seek and follow the guidance of God's inner call, guarantees a life of no regrets.

For each of us, regardless of where we are stuck, the road is one, the direction is one, the destination is one. Let us at least understand where we are headed: out of our heads, into the wilds of the soul's inner world, into the kingdom of Oneness. Like the Jews who wandered the Sinai in search of the Promised Land, we are destined to cross the desert of our own fruitless delusions, arriving at last at the realization of Self. Whether it takes forty years or forty million, we are headed Home.

I feel better already.

HOW REASONABLE IS REASON?

Hundreds of years ago, as we slowly emerged from the Dark and Middle Ages, reason became the engine for driving our development. From the 17th century onward, great strides were made in the sciences and mathematics. Modern philosophy was born, based on rational thought and logical methods of discovery. Rene Descartes declared from inspiration, "I think, therefore I am," and we found in ourselves an expanded sense of self-worth and capability. We began to explore beneath the surface of what was apparent.

As old ways of seeing our world gave way to brighter ideas, reason was viewed as the means to solve whatever might be improved. And anyone could apply it. Reason was not restricted to a favored caste or upper class. To paraphrase Paramhansa Yogananda, the thoughts that lead us to reason are universally rooted. We access them according to our level of consciousness, regardless of our social station in life.

Unfortunately, however, reason comes with a weakness. It depends on us to agree that what is reasonable is the same for all, which it never is. Reason tends to be fluid. People see it in relation to their own ideals and conditions. Hindus, Muslims, and Catholics, for instance, might find a number of each other's religious views to be out of step with their own "reasonable" beliefs. And needless to say, the degree of difference can lead to all sorts of trouble, even war.

Reason is a fabulous tool for helping good things to happen if kept from the taint of egoic interference. We need reason to get from point A to B, to get value for what we spend, to get wisdom from what we experience, and just to get through the day. But reason follows feeling, which can lead it into peril. Reasoning that emanates from emotion is probably not in alignment with the forces of cause and effect, and we are then apt to make a mess of what we have intended, and sometimes a mess of ourselves.

Overindulgence in a favorite desire, for example—like eating too many sweets or buying more goodies than we can really afford—is going to result in being sorry that we didn't stop at a reasonable point of enjoyment. We are all reasonable people, but I dare say not all the time. Delusion continues to outwit us until we learn self-control.

So, the question becomes: Is there any other tool that is more reliable than reason at discerning what works and what doesn't?

Meditators know of such a tool, which is intuition. But it comes with a caveat too. If you are going to act on intuition, you have to be sure it's the real McCoy and not just what an underlying desire wants it to be?

Maybe it makes more sense to stick with reason. Let's have a look.

The channel to true intuitive guidance is open when the conscious mind is elevated to a superconscious state. It literally connects a person to the Source of wisdom and its ways. But the mind must be still. If it is restless with desires, worries, or dozens of things to do, the voice of intuition will drown in the feverish noise of one's fidgety thoughts. How many whispers of higher guidance do we fail to hear each day because of being too busy to pause and listen? And how much further along would we be, on the path to both worldly success and spiritual progress, if we took the time to be inwardly quiet with our radio receivers tuned to the static-free channel of divine communication? Self-control is imperative.

Can reason lead us to intuition? It is not, after all, an intellectual process. But in one sense, yes it can, and Yogananda gave us the perfect prayer as we strive to acquire it. "I will reason, I will will, I will act; but guide Thou my reason, will, and activity."

Intuition is a two-way interaction. Our part is one of self-effort and surrender. We offer to do our best in whatever we pursue, taking care to evaluate what is right and dharmic to do in the first place. Then we ask God and Guru to show us the way, surrendering to them the result of our efforts, whether or not we manage to succeed as planned. Reason, combined with self-offering, thus becomes an invitation to bestow on us what reason alone cannot: access to higher guidance.

The trouble with reason is that it is born of the mind, just as the trouble with having a mind makes us prone to take our own advice. One of my favorite excuses for things going wrong is the same in every language: "I don't know how this happened. It seemed like such a good idea at the time!" All of us know about that one from experience.

In America's football Super Bowl—the biggest annual sporting event in the nation, watched on TV around the world by over a billion people—an astonishing moment occurred in the game played in 2015. With less than a minute to go, the Seattle Seahawks needed a touchdown to win. They were on the New England Patriot's one-yard line with four downs to score, so close to victory that no one, not even the Patriot players, could have dreamed the Seahawks would fail to run the ball that final distance and celebrate as the season's champions. But the coach called for the quarterback to throw a pass, which completely surprised everyone. The ball was deflected and intercepted by a Patriot's player, and suddenly the team that had been certain to lose was the team that won. Reacting in utter disbelief, Seahawk fans and pundits around the world immediately went ballistic. "What was the coach thinking???" All he could say was, "It seemed like a good idea at the time."

Reason is at the root of countless decisions every day that turn into disasters. Some of these make terrific stories later, causing little harm except for an awful few moments of public embarrassment. Swami Kriyananda used to tell a funny one on himself that was quite a gem. Back in the days of cassette recorders, he bought one and had it with him that night at a symphony at Carnegie Hall in New York, which holds about 3000 people. As the orchestra played, he thought to test the recorder's range and quality by carefully slipping it out of his pocket, unseen by anyone. In the next two seconds, three things happened at once. The orchestra came to a pause between two of the symphony's movements, Swamiji hit the "Play" button accidentally instead of "Record," and what everyone in the audience suddenly heard at full volume was the loud voice of the salesman that afternoon demonstrating the machine's audio proficiency: "Testing 1-2-3. Testing 1-2-3...!!!"

But many "reasonable" plans that go awry are not humorous in the least, especially the ones that miscalculate whether it is safe to proceed. The state of strife in today's world also provides ample evidence that one person's view of reason can be the launching pad for karmic bombs of all sorts.

Life is a test that nonetheless offers us tools to overcome the problems it presents. Meditation, intuition, and reason to a lesser extent, are among those tools to help us advance beyond the ways of constant trial and error to new levels of skill as we travel this path to Self-realization. Our assignment is to learn how to use them well, because when we do, God's grace and Guru's grace flow to us increasingly.

Everyone wants to be happy. We literally spend our lives in pursuit of that one goal. But who can keep it from drifting away? One moment we have it, and the next it is gone like sand through a sieve. Tune *in* to your *intuition*, the masters say. Stop looking under every rock for clues that reveal where to find what you are seeking. Those clues are right inside you, where the Source of them is waiting to show you the way. Tune in and listen. Intuition is there. God is there. Bliss is there. We should be there too.

FORM, FUNCTION AND FREUD

Oh, the complexities born of intelligent life!

If asked to defend his infamous deeds, Al Capone would surely have claimed to be a daring crusader—a freedom fighter of sorts—regrettably misunderstood by the less courageous. Like any ambitious entrepreneur, and not unlike the rest of us either, he believed in his goals and in what was needed to reach them. It's funny how people's doubts, to whatever extent they arise, seldom involve the merit of their own motives. In our minds we are serving the greater good even when self-absorbed.

In light of this not-so-startling fact, how can we ever hope to "Give peace a chance," and why in the world do we still look to politicians to lead the way? Tiresome rhetoric and volumes of legislation will never accomplish the feat. Can you imagine Al and his gang renouncing their illicit activities because of some new federal law?

Truly, we are a scattered lot in terms of evolution. Much of what seems to divide us into Al Capones and Mother Teresas and every character-type in between, is our past-life karma that carries over to this one. Some folks arrive with a ton of the abject variety, and whether they cope with reducing the load is always an uncertain issue. Furthermore, beyond this initial karmic stamp, we are faced with a host of other intrusive factors that are likely to have a say in who we become: parental, social, and peer-group conditioning in particular.

In short, our field of dreams is mined with explosives: words and definitions, rules and regulations, reason and responsibilities, and insurmountable mountains of empirical data. These are not wrong in themselves, except to the extent of reflecting a limited consciousness, which lacks direct experience of the Divine. Therein lies the source of our delusions, disguised as knowing.

Evidence of this can be seen in the relativism we substitute for truth. When man turns for assurance to his own systems alone, the only assurance that emerges is that of mutable standards for determining what is right. Too often our logic-and-information-based ways are derived from merely what we see, hear, feel, taste, and smell. And as no two minds will consistently interpret sensory input the same, how can we expect that neighbors of assorted traditions, mindsets, and relative points of view will ascend to a state of enduring agreeability? The odds in favor of this are probably less than none.

Our senses, after all, cannot testify to any event outside the scope of their own finite frontier. Nor can the human intellect refer an extra-sensory event anywhere but to its own records and files, which are "sensibly" assembled. In other words, we are bound by our analytical methods to arrive at solutions that sooner or later must fail. To believe that our brains can lead us to the Promised Land of harmonious living is just pure folly.

All of this begs the question: Why do our misadventures seem so magnetic? Given our reasoning abilities, one would think we would readily avoid the making of bonehead mistakes, not to mention repeating them hundreds of times. It appears to me that in driving headlong for happiness, as we are wont to do, we not only tend to miss the proper exit, we fail to recognize dangerous and dead-end roads when we find ourselves on them. Worse yet, we tend to institutionalize the directions that lead us astray.

Our confusion seems to commence and persist with the rules and laws—those endless maps—we invent as we ramble on. If one proves ineffective, we layer another on top. And so, in classic inverted fashion, rather than focus on whether a rule or law is likely to work, we first commit it to paper and ink—to a kind of solid form, that is—and then we impose it on the public at large. Finally, after the fact, we hurl bundles of money at it to make it function as planned. This is followed by wondering why it continues to function badly, or else not even noticing that it does.

Cutting to the chase, the problem for most of us Westerners stems from being persuaded that what we call reality is real. Unlike our Eastern elders, we hasten to organize life's illusions into patterns of ostensible intelligence that we have merely dreamed up. In imagining that security, for example, can exist in rules, laws, systems, and structures, we rush to create as many of these as our personal and public governance can manage. Or should I say *mis*manage? Rules, laws, systems and structures cannot give birth to function any more than a cart can precede the horse assigned to pull it. Unless in attunement with Natural Law, no policy or procedure can accomplish its full intent. More likely it will generate as many new issues as it remedies.

In his bold and insightful book, *Hope For A Better World*, Swami Kriyananda examines the elemental thoughts that for centuries have shaped us. Without reproach, he lays bare the flawed ideas on which we have based our very socialization. From the seminal teachings of Plato to the psychological investigations of Freud, he carefully notes the disconnects that we have overlooked in subscribing to many of the concepts that guide our lives. The likes of Machiavelli, Malthus, Adam Smith, Hegel, and Darwin have left us with incomplete scientific conclusions, which we have cemented in place at our culture's foundation. None of these influential men, brilliant as they were, went far enough in their thinking to realize the greater scope of what they studied. Darwin may have been partly correct in proposing "survival of the fittest," but with regard to humankind, he simply missed the boat in surmising that survival is our ultimate drive and that "fittest" is mainly an expression of might.

It is happiness we seek, and the fittest are those who recognize where it resides: in cooperative instead of competitive pursuits, in the elevation of mind to a spiritual rather than material perspective, in the peace of non-attachment to come-what-may.

Is it enough to be released of subconscious repressions, as Freud in effect asserted? Is that how freedom and happiness are achieved? The chances are slimmer than slim that hours or years on a therapist's couch would have groomed Al Capone to become Chicago's poster boy for model civic behavior. Sadly, as even modern psychiatry's rare successes reveal, the patient remains self-absorbed. His prison may be a roomier cell than before, but its bars are there all the same. Individual freedom expands only as one's concern for himself is cast away. It finds a healthy soil in which to grow when "What's in it for me?" is replaced by considering "What is the right thing to do?"

Kriyananda praises Freud for observing the extent to which our mental processes are concealed from our awareness. To scorn him for not discovering more would be, as he says, like criticizing Columbus for not describing California. But clearly the ideals of peace and love cannot take root in a Freudian strategy for healing. Nor in the theories of other intellectual figures who dominate our history's turbulent past. Until we expand our sympathies in lieu of our selfish ambitions, the means to a better world will be on hold.

Other "untils" are imperative too. Until we heed what works and surrender with humility our mistakes. . . Until we deconstruct the dogmas and creeds that set us apart, giving rise instead to our souls' aspirations. . . Until we accept that our brains are mere receivers, not the source of our insights and inventions. . . Until we forego our addiction to rules and other lifeless applications of reason, which only embolden the reckless and rebellious to disobey them. . . Until we acknowledge that when people's beliefs are based on egoic desires, none will escape corruption. . . Until we allow simplicity, moderation and service to guide our living. . . only then will we put an end to our self-indulgent longings that lead us astray.

BE THOU A YOGI

In the Bhagavad Gita, India's magnificent scripture, there's a mystical verse, the meaning of which is not easily understood. Lord Krishna, speaking to his disciple Arjuna, says, "That which is night for the unenlightened is day for the yogi. And that which is day for ordinary people is night for the yogi-seer."*

These words present us with a puzzle, and we have to look beneath their surface to solve it. Krishna is saying that what may seem real to us—we who see the world mainly with our limited senses—becomes *unreal* at a higher level of consciousness. As you and I move through our days, we rely on our conscious mind to analyze what we experience, helping us navigate the course of what we encounter. The yogi, however, has little interest in such mental or physical gymnastics. He (or she) looks to the "inner reality" for the guidance and answers he needs. And what he finds in that state of higher awareness nourishes him completely.

Well, that's interesting, but is it practical for people like you and me? Is it even possible? You and I live in a world that demands our daily attention and our outward activity if we expect to sustain ourselves. We are not yet so advanced that we can ignore the needs of our bodies, the need to put food on the table for ourselves and our families, the need to provide for the education and welfare of our children. We have responsibilities. Night and day for us are busy times of striving to make ends meet.

Can we still become yogis without losing sight of what we have to do on a daily basis? How can we be in this world without having it dictate the terms of our engagement with it?

When the ordinary person closes his eyes, what does he see? Not much. Mostly he closes his eyes to go to sleep. But what does the yogi see behind closed eyes? He sees light. He is fully awake to an infinitely marvelous reality beyond even the imagination of the ordinary person. Does he lose his worldly bearings? On the contrary, he is able to relate effectively to every facet of his life, both inward and outward, because nothing upsets him or pulls him out of

* Chapter 2, verse 69

his super-conscious understanding of what this life is about. It's about accepting and loving all that is—*everything*—as coming from God.

Well, that sounds lovely too, but where's the proof? We're very partial to factual evidence. Where's the science that verifies that life is about learning unconditional love, and learning that whatever comes is coming from God for our spiritual good? The proof we want can be found in one place only: in the laboratory of our own experience. We, individually, are the experiment in which the truth of our own highest potential can be revealed to us.

Agreeing with this, however, does not make it happen. We have to be willing to surrender ourselves to the actual experimental process and thereby allow the proof to be shown. That is what is most difficult to do, because all of our habits, attachments, and desires are certain to conspire against us, distracting us from the inward, meditative process that is the way forward.

Krishna, in the next verse, then tells us what we have to do to rise from the level of ordinary people to that of a true yogi. "Contentment is his who, like the vast ocean, absorbs into himself all the rivers of desire."

This harkens to the very essence of Patanjali's definition of yoga: *Yogas chitta vritti nirodh.* Yoga is the neutralization of the vortices of feeling, the cancellation of our ego-driven desires. *Chitta* are the biased feelings of the heart—our egoic likes and dislikes—that lead us into delusion and thus into worldly bondage. Until these "rivers of our desire" cease to flow from us into outward manifestation, we cannot know contentment.

Well, that's a bit depressing. What about all those movies I like, and my favorite foods, and the pleasures of getting away on vacation? Can't I be content to be contented just part of the time? What's wrong with that?

Well, there's nothing wrong with that except for what is certain to follow: some measure of disappointment, or worse, when the temporary pleasure I have experienced comes to its finite end, as it must. Just as night follows day, and as up cannot exist without down, worldly pleasures are counterbalanced also. Surely it is wiser to aim for that perspective—the yogi's perspective—that does not sacrifice joy when tests and trials arrive.

I grant you, this may seem very hard at first, because we have been extremely well conditioned to believe that our worldly desires and pursuits are the best means we have to be happy. But Krishna repeatedly reminds us not to be fooled by that kind of thinking. Think not to get, but to give. Think not to resist what is ours to receive, but how to make the most of it instead. Think not to possess, but to enjoy and let go. It's all a dance of the four A's: Attitude, Attunement, Acceptance and Action.

Along with our free will to choose the direction of our lives, God gave us the ability to choose wisely: the power to discriminate, which is more than the power to reason. Discrimination is a gift of the soul's intuitive connection to Spirit. Reason can be manipulated by desire, but discrimination is born of attunement to God's will and His ways. To discriminate carefully is to channel those rivers of our worldly preoccupations into our calm, oceanic center, where they can be absorbed and disappear.

The path to becoming a yogi is a lot about *neti, neti:* not this, not that. Everything we desire that is born of the ego needs to be understood as *neti, neti.* Can we still enjoy the things of this earth? Yes, of course, and we should, but with the love of God, with discrimination, with right attitude and with non-attachment. That is the key to entering the yogi's luminous "inner reality." It's the key to finding contentment in every circumstance. And it's the key to knowing that what we outwardly see as day is a dream, a dream that cannot begin to compare with the Light that shines like a thousand suns behind the closed eyes of one whose desire is to realize God.

Krishna says to Arjuna, "Be thou a yogi." The message is meant for us.

"Where are we?" the stranger beside me asked. "Is this Hell?"

"No," I replied. "This is the Vast Mundane. It's not so bad. You get used to it."

"How is it different than Hell?"

"The fire here isn't as hot," I explained. "Here we only simmer for our sins."

The line to the ticket window was long, and I struck up a conversation with the fellow behind me. We made the usual small talk, and then I asked what he did for a living.

"I'm self-employed," he replied with a slightly superior air. In his hand was a finely tooled stick.

"What do you do?" I inquired further.

"I work at beating the darkness into light," he said, showing me the stick.

"That's a nice one, all right. Does it do the trick?"

"Not yet," he said with a little sigh. "You have to be persistent. These things take a lot of practice. Rome wasn't built in a day."

"Your commitment is impressive," I remarked, "but meanwhile, how do you make ends meet?"

"Oh, I have another job too," he said. "I'm a life coach."

CHAPTER 4

Truth

"He who binds to himself a joy

Doth the winged life destroy.

But he who kisses the joy as it flies

Lives in Eternity's sunrise."

William Blake

Everyone takes delivery of the unwanted. You don't have to sign for it; it arrives in your mailbox or inbox, in your hand or in your face, unbidden except as a consequence for some previous karmic mistake. The trick is to find within it the hidden message of love and opportunity it carries, knowing that nothing is not as it needs to be, and to meet its challenge with willingness and corrective action.

What makes this difficult, of course, is our conditioned resistance to everything we dislike and seemingly did not invite. Required is a change of attitude, which starts with acceptance of change itself, which means letting go of thinking that we deserve better than what we received.

The undesirable arrives, by degrees, as a creeping inevitability or sudden ambush. It may be that which has been feared and postponed, or a karmic detonation without warning. Worst cases come with chaos and confusion.

To find the hidden message in the unwanted, you have to know that nothing but a calm approach is going to reveal its wisdom and allow its guidance to be gathered. Chaos and confusion are not pathology. They are part of the path, to be calmly encountered, resolved and left behind. You must give disturbance a home before you can evict it.

The goal is to make of yourself the true you who is not who you are yet. If the journey were an easy one, we would all be that already.

To meet the dawn, you must endure the night. And if you endure it rightly, you will find it not so dark as tales tell. It is but a length of time that is certain to pass, faster as you lose your fear of the noises it makes. Take heart and see it through. Even in the deep of it, there are stars.

Can you jump without coming down? After every soaring slam-dunk, even Michael Jordan returned to the floor. So, why do we think we can ride a wave of excitement without finally sliding down its face, sometimes landing in disrepair beneath its crashing break? Whether in a storm of thrills and spills or merely a series of rolling swells and retreats, every wave must balance its peak with a trough. Better to seek the deep water that does not toss and churn.

AND THE TRUTH SHALL SET YOU FREE

Devi tells a funny story about her son Kalidas when he was maybe three or four years old. He had discovered her stock of vitamins, which were hidden away in her closet, precisely to avoid what might occur if he should happen upon them. Fascinated by the different colors and shapes, Kalidas unscrewed the lids on the bottles and poured the contents onto the floor, blending them into a lovely tossed salad of capsules, gels, and tablets. Then suddenly it struck him that he could be in trouble, so he took the initiative. He went to his mother and firmly announced, "Mommy, I didn't do nothing." Devi responded, "Oh, and just *where* is the nothing you didn't do?" "In the closet," he said, "but I didn't do it."

Maybe as we get older, we get a bit more inventive at concealing our mischief, but the fact is, no one gets away with being untruthful. There is always at least an adverse spiritual effect, which is ultimately the costliest effect of all.

"Truth will out," we have heard since we were kids. But still there are times when we dearly wish that it would stay bottled up. Those are the times when the ego is loath to admit a foolish mistake that would publicly stain its coveted reputation. It is sure to have an excuse at hand, or it may even want us to lie to avoid being punished or embarrassed.

Resorting to little "white" lies is commonly egoic too. It is only natural, of course, that we like to make the best impression in every situation, so maybe we exaggerate a bit when talking about ourselves, or we change the facts of a story to make ourselves look smarter or more skillful. Or maybe we say that our grand-mother died, and that's why we didn't show up to do the job we said we would. (It's a running joke in India how often a close relative will suddenly pass away, only to reappear a few days later in the very same body as before, healthy and ready to die again as needed!)

Accepting the truth is, in truth, the only useful way to live, *because it guarantees a happier life*, and because resisting the truth is certain to make a mess of things sooner or later. When you abide in the truth, there's no other strategy required. You don't have to think about how to cover your tracks, because there's nothing to hide.

There are three words in the English language that begin with the letter D that can get us into a whole lot of trouble: Desire, Delusion, and Dishonesty. Regret-tably, there are plenty of people out there—in business, in politics, in relation-ships—whose dishonesty is habitual. They connive to take advantage of others, or to promote their own unwarranted ambitions, and often they succeed. Or so they believe. But dishonesty is bound to backfire, if not at that moment then at a future time, for God is not asleep on the job. A consequence will come to pass.

Devi's story about her son is told mostly for laughs, but the daily news is awash in tales of intentional fabrications that are not humorous at all, and some of the most egregious ones reflect on the state of our religious values and affairs. A major part of Paramhansa Yogananda's mission in the West was to restore "original Chris-tianity," which, as he said, had devolved into "Churchianity;" in other words, into a dishonest representation of what Christ had taught.

In the case of the Catholic Church, for example, it has supported two funda-mental falsehoods in order to promote and maintain its position of supreme author-ity. It has purged from the New Testament references made by Jesus to reincarna-tion* as the process by which we advance toward Self-realization, and thus it has also

---

* In the sixth century, the Church was divided over the issue of reincarnation. Western bishops in Rome believed in the pre-existence of the soul, while Eastern bishops did not. Emperor Justinian, who controlled the Eastern Church, was against the doctrine of reincarnation, and in 553 A.D. he convened the Fifth Ecumenical Council to further his agenda. Only six bishops of the Western Church were present; from the Eastern Church, there were 159. It was at this meeting that pre-existence of the soul was voted out of Church doctrine, and Jesus' references to it in the New Testament were summarily removed. Pope Vigilius protested this turn of events, demanding equal representation between Eastern and Western bishops. Justinian not only ignored the Pope, he had him imprisoned and persecuted.

denied that we, as individuals, do not even need the Church itself, its clergy, or its religious laws to achieve the soul's liberation.

Much good has been done by the Catholic Church and others, but when any institution places itself above the highest principles and truths on which it was founded—whether it be a government, a corporation, a charity, or a church—it loses its moral compass.

We all know about karma. You cannot outfox or escape it. As it says in the Bible, "Be not deceived, God is not mocked. For whatsoever a man soweth, that shall he also reap."

But God is also generous, and when we are truthful, even when we willingly admit to a serious transgression, there will always be a karmic blessing that follows in some form or other. At the least there is a sense of mental relief, the sense of a cleansing.

When we think of what it means to be truthful, most of us would say that it means to *tell* the truth, especially to ourselves. But that is only part of the definition. It also means to accept what we cannot change. Think how often we wish that things were different than we find them. "I wish I were taller. . . I wish I were younger. . . I wish I didn't have to deal with this traffic. . . I wish my boss was nicer to me. . . I wish I hadn't dropped that rock on my foot."

Only in facing reality *as it is* can we begin to make it what it *ought to be*. Just like Arjuna in the Bhagavad Gita, we have to be willing to work with every circumstance as it comes, no matter how difficult it may be, such as a serious injury, the loss of a job, or an *actual* death in the family. Challenges like these arise in everyone's life, and when they do, we cannot *undo* what has already taken place. We have to move on or suffer.

Another story from Swami Kriyananda's life illustrates exactly the kind of attitude we need to develop. Many years ago in California, Swamiji invited a group of devotees to join him on a skiing trip. As they drove to their destination, it started to snow. Everyone was in a joyful mood, when suddenly the car hit a patch of ice and spun out of control, crashing into a Grehound bus. Fortunately, no one was hurt, but the car was wrecked. What had been a happy holiday excursion appeared to be ruined. And not only that, they were stuck out in the cold without transportation.

You can imagine how most people would react to that situation. They would catapult into a brooding mood, complaining that what had happened was terribly unfair. This would lead to anger, adding further insult to their distress. They would hire a car to take them back home, and there they would spend the next days or weeks sulking and wishing they could change the result.

So here is what Swamiji did. He arranged for a truck to tow the car away, then everyone got on the bus, and off they went to enjoy their holiday outing. When a passenger on the bus asked Swamiji how he could simply walk away from such a loss, Swamiji said with a smile, "A week from now the car will be fixed, or I will get another one, and my life will be back to normal. So why should I waste a week being sad when I can choose to be happy right now?" Everyone had a wonderful time skiing, and the whole incident got resolved later on.

Life is full of twists and turns. We never know what the next moment will bring, but we can be sure, especially if it assails our composure, that it is a gift in the garb of inconvenience, a chance to make real progress against an imbedded resistance.

In denial, there is suffering. In acceptance of truth, and in truthfulness, suffering has nowhere to find a way in.

ON THE TRAIL OF TRUTH AND TREASURE

One of the hallmarks of human intelligence is our ability to reason. The more reasonable we are, the more successful we tend to be. But reason has a limited range of reliability. Its intellectual system of analysis does not deal so well with questions like "What is this life all about?" or "Why is it so hard to stay happy?"

If you are a person of faith, I suppose the ultimate question is, "What is this game that God is making us play, and why is He doing it?"

Reason cannot answer these questions in a verifiable way. We want to know the mind of God, but that is not within our capacity to grasp. We can talk about it, and we do, but its depth is beyond the reach of our comprehension.

And the plot continues to thicken. As if to add an extra measure of toil and sweat to our lives, it seems that God has hidden a number of mystical truths from us to make the game last longer. Douglas Adams, author of *The Hitchhiker's Guide to the Galaxy*, had a theory as to why it is so hard to beat the odds that are against us. He postulated that if everyone figured out how the universe functions and what it is for, it would instantly disappear and be replaced by something even stranger than before. He also had a theory that this has already happened!

Guided by reason alone, almost anyone would have to conclude that God has hidden a lot from us. We have further evidence of this in Jesus' words, "Cast not pearls before swine," meaning that it would be reckless to disclose a higher truth to someone who is not yet ready to hear it. From such people, yes, God has surely hidden certain verities which they would neither understand nor act upon in a beneficial manner.

On the other hand, we have revelations and testimony from hundreds of saints and ascended masters who, throughout history, have led us to esoteric truths that reason leaves unresolved. Ultimately, it becomes a matter of where you put your faith: in someone's analysis of truth based on mere physical evidence, or in revelations of those, based on actual experience, that reason can neither explain nor explain away?

I have no doubt that saints and ascended masters are the ones to trust in matters of how to deal with life's most fundamental questions. But that said, it is easy to get confused because this world, much of the time, is a very strange place to have landed. Consider, for example, the events that make up most of the daily news, the stresses that undermine most workplace environments, and all of those egoic desires that complicate our ability to live in peace and in joy. If there is a way out of this mess—and thankfully there is—the fact remains that we don't get a lot of help from the world itself.

What we have here is a treasure hunt, and most people don't even know what the treasure is. They think it is something outside themselves that involves the correct application of clever thinking. They rely largely on their emotions to tell them what they want, and if they manage to get it, they soon discover that its flavor doesn't last, so they start the whole exhausting process again. . . and again and again and again.

Admittedly, the clues that lead to life's real treasure can often be rather difficult to read. That's because our society, with its largely Western influence, is presenting us with values and goals that are shallow and short-sighted, and thus people are led astray of what truly matters, of what could make them happy now and forever.

Years ago there was a popular TV show called *Mission Impossible*. It has since inspired a series of truly "impossible" Tom Cruise movies. But in the earlier TV version, before the advent of computerized special effects, the stories were almost believable, and the opening scene was always much the same. A phone would ring in a telephone booth in some remote location, and special agent Jim Phelps would be there to answer it and receive his assignment. A voice on the other end of the line would say, "Your mission, Jim, if you choose to accept it, is to…" well, to do whatever was needed in the next 60 minutes—between commercials—to save the world from some fiendish plot. It was all very cool and suspenseful.

But in our daily reality, the assignment for us is not so easily scripted. We have to answer that phone every morning, and here is the instruction we receive: "Your mission, dear one, is to figure out what the treasure is, where it is, and how to secure it. It is highly probable that since you are now seeking truth instead of people's approval, many of them will be trying to shoot you down. Oh, and by the way, there is no option here. This is your assignment, like it or not. You can put it off as long as you choose, but as you will find at the end of your life, death is not an escape hatch. Until you make that treasure your own, you will have to return again and again until you finish the job."

So here we are. The good news is, we have been in this world long enough for the weirdness of it to seem quite natural. The bad news is, that because it seems quite natural, we tend to gravitate to its many forms of distraction: TV, the Internet, shopping malls, sporting events, and other kinds of mere entertainment. That's okay, it just isn't getting us where we really want to be.

Back in the 1950s, there was a wacky TV game show called *Beat the Clock*, and it was one of my favorites when I was kid. A contestant would race against time to accomplish a series of totally silly maneuvers in order to win a prize, such as balancing a bowl of eggs on his head while climbing a ladder to ring a bell, or running through an obstacle course of various hurdles and hoops, wearing big, floppy clown feet.

Years later, after a couple of decades in the advertising business, it occurred to me that a lot of what we do every day is just about as silly, except that now we take it so seriously, especially the game of getting ahead, of getting more, and of getting noticed. Some days we win a little prize, and some days that bowl of eggs on our head goes crashing to the floor. In either case, these pressures leave us looking for ways to unwind. What most people choose is some sort of sensory or emotional pleasure, which is perfectly understandable. Alas, however, none of that escapism is going to set us free. Until we go into the silence, into the soul, into the experience of who we truly are, it's as if we are strapped in a rollercoaster car, going up and down, around and around, on a wild ride of swerves and sudden plunges.

When you witness the world objectively, the constant repetition of our rollercoaster behavior hardly supports the claim that we are the planet's most intelligent species. Nor does it lead to the treasure we are meant to find. The real mystery here is not whether God hides the truth, but why people spend so much time and effort trying to ignore it. Clearly, most folks would rather do what everyone else is doing than make a change for the better. Conformity for the sake of conformity is a kind of national disease, especially when it takes us in the opposite direction of where our bliss awaits, in God-realization.

Much of what I appreciate about Ananda is that within its membership there is so much less conformity and rollercoaster behavior going on. We are certainly not immune to the ego's interference in our lives, but we're consciously focused on moving in the right direction—inward instead of outward—and I am deeply grateful to be surrounded by that positive, progressive, and more productive influence.

This world will no doubt remain a strange place in many ways, but Ananda offers an antidote to its miseries and mistaken ideals. We know where the truth lies. God has not hidden it from us. It lies in the heart. . . in plain view.

CHAPTER 5

Faith

"The grace of God is a wind that is always blowing."

Sri Ramakrishna

Such As We Are

Mark Twain was one of those complex characters who wrestled with the concept of a just and loving God. Writing over a hundred years ago, he was probably unfamiliar with the word *karma*, but like most of us at times, he wondered how far he go in giving in to certain urges and behaviors without incurring a costly karmic debt. A quote of his says it all. "Some people," he said, "are troubled by passages in the Bible which they do not understand. What troubles me are the passages I *do* understand!"

One of those passages might have been this one: "'Your ways are not My ways', sayeth the Lord." This could have made him a bit uneasy, because Twain was not always ready to choose the Lord's ways. Nor are we. We have habits, moods, ambitions, attachments, and desires that tend to compete with living a spiritual life. When the world is calling to us with attractive distractions, the Lord's ways often become inconvenient, and we put them on hold to indulge our whims and yearnings.

How often do we also wish that things were not as we have caused them to be, and that we could find an escape clause in the karma that we have thereby drawn to ourselves?

Quotes like the one of Twain's are intended to get a laugh, but they're born of a certain anxiety. Our laughter is an acknowledgement that we have been there too, wishing we could change what we cannot, knowing deep down it is we who must change. This whole earthly manifestation is God's phenomenal dream, and God has given us free choice in how the dream unfolds, enabling us to bless or curse ourselves with every decision and action we undertake.

The predicament for us, of course, is that God's dream doesn't seem like a dream at all. It has a definable reality. Trying to ignore what that is, arguing with God about how he has arranged it, or pleading with Him to give us a break because dealing with it just seems too hard, is not going to get us any farther along than we are now. The path to freedom can be traveled as fast or as slowly as we choose, but we cannot choose to avoid it and still find our way Home.

Our challenges range from insignificant to severe, and they are incessant. Some of us may apparently have it easier than others, but for each of us the biggest problem of all is universally and equally shared. It's a problem that is so obvious, it is easy to overlook: *We're still here!* If we were free of delusion, we would be somewhere else, immersed in a sea of Bliss. But we're not. We are where we are, as we are, back again to have another crack at making progress.

In a popular year-end class by Nayaswami Shivani, she talks about what happens when we die. Her information has been confirmed repeatedly by people who went through a near-death experience, but who were ultimately returned to life for one reason or another. While on the other side, they said they had to appear for a life review, and in that review two questions were asked. There was no mention of how many hours they had worked late at the office, how much wealth they had acquired, or whether they had excelled at any particular skill. What the reviewer wanted to know was this: What did you learn, and how much did you love? That's all. What did you learn, and how much did you love?

How would you answer those questions today if you suddenly found yourself on the other side of life? Would you be as prepared as you'd like to be? I suspect that all of us would have to say that we could have done more to be ready, that we could have been more loving.

It is odd that although we aspire to attain our soul's freedom, we spend much of our lives in pursuits of limitation instead, striving for gains that tether us to the fleeting diversions and disappointments of chasing our worldly wishes. Unwittingly, the glutton for pleasure becomes the glutton for punishment as well.

All of us, like Mark Twain, would gladly delete a few of the Bible's more demanding passages from our curriculum. We wouldn't mind if there were fewer difficult people and situations to contend with as well. But that's not how the dream has been designed, and you can be sure that whatever upsets you is there because (1) you have something to learn from the experience, and (2) you need to apply more love to make it better, because love conquers all.

Patience is needed too. Consider the seed that lies in the shell of an acorn. It may aspire to be a mighty oak, and indeed, the oak is already fully contained in that tiny kernel. But the seed cannot fulfill its potential in a mere leap of faith.

Slowly and daily, it has to do the requisite work to become a sprout, then a twig, a sapling, and so on. These are inescapable stages of development, and for us the story is the same. We look to the goal, but we cover the distance one step at a time—one less binding desire at a time—appreciating and relishing the journey itself.

As we act to free ourselves from our limiting habits, desires, and attachments, we set in motion an energy that sweeps away resistance in the same way that a swift river sweeps away eddies of debris along its banks. As it gathers momentum, that energy draws to itself greater inspiration, more joy, and accumulating success. But once again, we have to do the work.

What did you learn, and how much did you love? In these two questions lies the total of what this life is about. Did you learn that people are more important than things, that right action leads to the right result, that selfless service is a magnet for inner bliss? Did you learn that God wants nothing from you but your love, expressed in all that you do?

This life is not as mysterious as we tend to make it. The trouble is, we try to have our way, which is not the way that "sayeth the Lord." When we get aboard the Lord's way, good things happen, growth occurs, and we lose our gluttonous taste for punishment too. All that it takes is loving all that is.

You Have God Already

Do you have trouble remembering your name? or where you live? or what your favorite pastimes are? Of course not. These recollections are important to us. Each of us has a mental file of memories that is central to our ideals and our identity. Some of these help us to navigate through each day, some fill us with gladness, and some are essential to our well-being.

I mention this, because it is quite amazing how easily we forget the most important thought of all: that we are children of the Light, endowed with divine consciousness, created by and of the Mind of God. We are not just flesh and bone. We are not the sum of our successes and failures. We are not our name, age, sex, or level of intelligence. We are the wondrous expression of our eternal souls.

Can you imagine anything more encouraging or uplifting? And yet, in the course of a difficult day, this probably never occurs to us. We forget that we are more than our human condition, that we are spiritual beings who are merely having a temporary human experience.

In Ananda's Festival of Light, Swami Kriyananda urges us to realize our soul's true nature when he says, "O children of Light, forsake the darkness... *know that forever you and He are one.*"

And still we manage to lose sight of that as soon as we hit a hard bump in the road. The reason is understandable. We're surrounded by a kind of craziness known as *maya*—delusion—and because it exists almost everywhere, it's easy to fall into its traps. Our lives are busy and sometimes even chaotic with many distractions. We have desires and ambitions. We have problems and responsibilities. We get upset. We get tired. There are days when the gravity that holds our feet to the ground seems to pull even more heavily downward on our hearts and minds.

As children of the Light, you would think we'd know better than to let our longings interfere with our higher guidance. But we are also human, and like Arjuna in the Bhagavad Gita, we have our karmic battles to fight before our soul's liberation is won. We, like him, are pitted against those familiar "cousins" of ours that cause us so much trouble: our habits, moods, emotions, desires, and attachments; and only we can decide if we want to fight harder now and win the war sooner, or retreat into the ego and wait much longer. Swami Kriyananda said many times that if we make the effort now, we can be *jivan muktas*—freed of ego-consciousness—by the time we reach the end of this incarnation.

Don't get me wrong, there are many wonderful things about this life: wonderful people, places and activities. But it is also a veil of tears, and lovelier realms await us when we have graduated from this one.

Years ago, when Tushti and I lived in Honolulu, we had the very good fortune to study karate with a former Japanese champion. We called him Shihan, a title of honor like Swami, and I believe he must have been a great swami in a previous life, a kind of samurai swami. Shihan was a very high soul, incredibly strong inside and out, yet equally humble and generous. He and Yogananda had a lot in common. No matter how strict he appeared, there was always a twinkle in his eye that was loving and delightful.

At the start of every karate class, we would line up at attention and bow as a way of declaring our readiness to receive and practice what Shihan would teach. Then he would ask in a booming voice, "How you feel today? You feel good? Okay. But maybe you feel tired or you have headache. That is even better, because now you must try harder. When enemy come, make no difference how you feel. If you no fight, maybe you die!"

I think about those last two sentences a lot. Shihan, in his broken English, was not just referring to the enemy as someone who wants to harm you. He, like Yogananda, was referring to every attractive delusion that pulls us off the path to our salvation. That is the real enemy. Maybe it is something that seems insignificant, like deciding to skip your meditation; or maybe it is more serious, like acting in a way that is not ethical. Even the slightest deviation from dharma diminishes our spirituality. That is why, "When enemy come, make no difference how you feel. If you no fight, maybe you die" to a golden chance you were given to be rid of a troublesome karma.

If you want to succeed against any challenge, you must meet it with a strong will and plenty of energy, no matter what. That's because you are not only a *child* of the Light, you must also be a *warrior* of the Light, just like Shihan or Swami Kriyananda. Life is a test of our inner resources. As devotees, we know that everything comes from God, that it happens for a purpose, and that it is meant for our spiritual growth.

Whether or not you succeed in overcoming every adversity, always remember what Yogananda emphatically repeated to his disciples: "Live in the thought that you have God already." You are divine. When that is your affirmation, and when you act from that awareness, nothing can stop your progress.

FINDING HAPPIER

Everyone wants to be happy. Having a happy day, a happy encounter, a happy life, is a universal desire. In a twisted way, this is even what gangsters and warlords want. But happiness is a very capricious condition. So, how do we get it, grow it, and keep it alive?

The answer to that question is actually an easy one, because we have it already. Happiness is the gold of our inner nature, buried under the surface of our outward ambitions and attachments. There is nothing to get, only a lot to get rid of. We are of Spirit, and Spirit is Bliss. Our task is simply to strip away the many layers of camouflage we have wrapped and covered our happiness in.

Whether we are aware of it or not, every choice we make, and every action we take, is aimed at being happy. It is only because our desires are mostly short-term and superficial that our happiness does not last. We live on the surface of who we are, missing out on the depth that is so much richer.

Although our choices and actions could be wiser, it is understandable why they are not. We've been taught to entrust our happiness to that which is outside ourselves, to invest in people and things that come and go. Clearly, nothing and no one endures. We are bound to lose what we have, including our mortal selves. And yet the inward alternative to this outward way of life gets little if any mention.

Alas, the outside world has no interest in nourishing our inner nature. It sees us as consumers, and expects us to act accordingly. Western society in particular is forever committed to selling us its finite dreams of material gain, dreams and gains that neither we nor it can long sustain.

That said, we have not seen the last of our worldly desires. I have my favorites too, and a few of them are as firmly attached as barnacles on a rock. But a few years ago I took a vow, and I will tell you more about that in a few paragraphs further down. Meanwhile, there's more to say about where and why we are stuck in a bind.

No one wants to suffer. Yet we have come to realize that worldly pleasures fade and die, leaving unpleasant gaps before more of the same can be found to replace what is gone. We don't seem to know a better way to live, and for many the unpleasant gaps become the prevailing norm. Soon, too, even our highs fall short of what we expect our happiness to be. Searching outside ourselves for people and things to make us happy inside, we invariably invite the opposite: periods of feeling unhappy and unfulfilled, wanting more from this limited world than it can provide.

A ship at sea, laden with heavy cargo, turns wide and slowly in changing its course. Likewise, laden with karma, we also tend to reverse direction slowly, even when stormy weather looms ahead and the promise of a happier life beckons from a brighter horizon. The habit of auto-pilot is hard to break, and this applies to our spiritual lives as well. Change takes effort, and it carries a sense of risk, especially when the quest for its reward demands greater discipline.

Change, effort, and discipline were themes that firmly held my attention on December 31, 2009. That was the night that some of us in Palo Alto launched ourselves into the coming New Year by taking a sacred vow, written by Swami Kriyananda. It's a vow recited in seeking to remove the signs of separation between oneself and God. The devotee aspires to make Self-realization the first and foremost purpose of his life. Those of us who took that vow—men and women alike—were joining a new order of spiritual renunciates, since known as the Nayaswami Order.

In the same manner that saffron is the color worn by swamis of the ancient tradition, we wear astral blue. This is to signify to others, and to remind ourselves, that we aim to end all sense of "I and mine," and to offer ourselves in selfless service to God and thus to others. Ours is an age of energy and higher consciousness. Its paradigm is no longer mechanistic or materialistic: hence the addition of *Naya* to the Order's name.

My wife Tushti and I took the vow together. This was a major decision, and like a few others in our marriage and within Ananda, a pattern could be seen. From my perspective, it looked like this: Tushti would climb to the top of a 10-meter diving platform, walk to the edge, look to make sure of water in the pool below, turn back to me and say, "I'm going to jump in. Are you coming too?"

Now, this is not my approach to a big move. I'm a bit afraid of heights in the first place, and I'm also rather compulsively analytical. I want to know how to cover that 10-meter distance with pauses here and there to ease the transition! A dive from that elevation, however, does not allow for mid-air adjustments. You go for it or you don't, and that final step over the edge of security and comfort is always the hardest one to take, even when you believe it's the right thing to do.

"What if the vow is more than I can live up to?" I pondered anxiously. "People will be watching. What if this dive ends in a great big bellyflop? *'Oooh, did you see that! He hit the water flat as a pancake! What was he thinking?'"*

Well, the leap was made, and it has given me much to be thankful for. I am certainly no poster boy for nayaswami comportment, but the vow is a nudge to be mindful of where my happiness truly lies, and that it grows as I grow with it. I know very well what my weaknesses are, and others who know me are aware of them too. So, what's to lose?

In becoming a nayaswami, my commitment has been to the journey more than its destination. Its direction is what matters most. We recognize at Ananda that each of us is dealing with karmic issues that may be very difficult to wrestle down, and we offer ourselves in tolerance and assistance to the cause of everyone's spiritual advancement. That makes for happier times.

Being happy is not about learning how, it's about unlearning to suffer. Dale Carnegie said it well: "Success is getting what you want. Happiness is wanting what you get." We all get the good and not so good delivered to us daily. When the not-so-good is received in the right spirit, suffering has nowhere to enter, and happiness presides.

IS GOD THE SOURCE OF EVIL TOO?

How did our universe come into being? Will science and religion ever find a way to agree on the answer? Probably not in my lifetime. One is overly committed to physical data and facts, the other to scriptural interpretation, which religious scholars themselves are unable to agree upon. And both dismiss the spiritual perspective, which is surely closer to the truth than either of them seems willing to consider.

Science favors the "Big Bang" theory, which seems to make sense as far as it goes, but still it leaves a missing piece of the puzzle. All of that elemental "stuff" that exploded into existence, where did it come from? We simply have to look deeper into this mystery than science is able to do.

In the Bhagavad Gita, Krishna says to Arjuna, "I am the light of the sun, the cosmic sound, the sustaining life." He does not say, "I *created* the sun, the sound, and the life," he declares that *"I am"* these things. In other words, the consciousness that is Krishna—that is God—pre-existed every atom and every unit of space that can be measured. And here's what is really incredible about Krishna's statement: If God became the universe, then God is in the seed that gave birth to you and me. He has not merely created us, He has *become* what you and I are today.

Now that poses another mystery, because we think of God as perfect, as goodness itself. But obviously that appraisal does not apply to everyone, perhaps not even to most of us. If God has become us, and if He is the perfection of goodness, how can we explain the many acts of terrorism and hatred that we see being committed? Why is God strapping bombs to His body and blowing Himself up on crowded streets, killing innocent people?

That question takes us into the strange and complex issue of our free will. God, we are told, gave us the freedom to behave as we choose. Does that mean He is also the satanic force that urges people to treat each other badly? to be selfish and greedy? to cheat and steal and lie? If God has become all things, the answer must be yes. He cannot be separate from evil. He must also exist in the thoughts and deeds of every wrong-doer.

No matter how you slice it, the concept of God's consciousness infused into every atom, and into every person, is difficult to grasp. This is a planet of seven billion personalities! Consider how different we are in our likes and dislikes, in our physical and emotional makeup, and in our beliefs. In religious matters alone, people's ideas range from insightful and wise to fundamentally ludicrous. And yet God has become them all.

If you try to make human sense of this—well, you simply cannot. Our ability to reason is just too limited to wrap itself around such an expansive notion. And I dare say that reason is not exactly applied with consistency when it comes to religious discussion and debate. Witness, for example, the countless number of wars that have been fought—and are being fought today—in the name of competing religious points of view.

As Swami Kriyananda said repeatedly, the only true authorities in terms of religious meaning are the ascended masters and saints, because they alone speak from personal *experience* of Divine communion. Anyone else, regardless of meaning well, has some degree of incomplete knowledge, some degree of ignorance. With incomplete knowledge, we tend to arrive at incomplete theories, such as the "Big Bang," which is not necessarily wrong; it simply does not go far enough to tell the whole story. For that you need a *super*conscious connection.

Let's get back to God as the source of what is bad as well as good. If God is One, with a capital O, and if there is no other One, as every avatar has declared, then the obvious answer is yes: God *did* become the satanic force and everything that it produces.

Well, good grief, why would He do such a thing?

The rest of this essay, if it is going to make sense to you, necessitates a willingness to think beyond the strictly scientific or religious outlook. With faith in the answer that spirituality gives us, let me see if I can make this comprehensible.

When God became the universe, He did so by means of His Consciousness, because that is what God is. He is Consciousness, which is the source of light, of energy and of all things material. God's Consciousness, which is infinite in its capacity to express Itself, vibrated outwardly from Its still-point, and from that vibration all potential objects and ideas came into being.

That initial vibration made a sound in the same way a tuning fork does, and that sound was the sound of AUM. It is from the AUM, depending upon the rate of its oscillation, that we have such things as suns and moons, rocks, plants, rocket ships, and the likes of you and me. The atoms that are holding you and me together simply vibrate at a faster rate than the atoms in the chairs we sit on, and thank goodness for that, or we'd crash to the floor!

A vibration moves back and forth like a pendulum, swinging equally in both directions. Thus, we have the birth and perpetual existence of duality, the invariable two-sidedness of all that is: night and day, high and low, hot and cold, pleasure and pain, etc. This two-sidedness requires that every concept, feeling, and thing must possess—in potential—its own opposite quality. And so, to the quality of goodness, we must also add that of evil.

Alas, 'tis true. God is the source of every such pairing we experience: good and evil, love and hate, wisdom and ignorance, order and chaos, happiness and sorrow. According to the Law of Vibration, which operates universally, not even He can change this, except to withdraw the totality of it back to its pre-"Big Bang" vibrational state (known in Hinduism as the Night of Brahma).

But why, if He loves us, would God set such a demanding system in motion?

Consider the main ingredient of an excellent story. It is the suspense that develops as the story moves along, the tension that arises between what is good and that which tries to defeat it. Think of the battle of Kurukshetra in the Bhagavad Gita. If the Pandavas had not been challenged by a very powerful army of egoic tendencies, it would have been a dull story indeed. We need strong and clever villains in order to appreciate the courage and strength that is needed to put them behind us. Heroes inspire us to do what they do, to be like them, and thus to move progressively closer to a life of true contentment.

God inserted Himself into the power of darkness so that we could see how magnificent is the power of light. Nobody wants to suffer, but most of us do because we have not yet learned the value of putting our energy 100 percent behind the quest for inner freedom. Suffering is the real villain, and we need it to remind us of where we are lacking in our commitment to seek peace, to seek joy, to seek the Light of God.

Life is remarkably simple. It is all about discovering what works and what doesn't. God does not punish us for the wrongs we commit; we punish ourselves by failing to change. This universe is God's dream. We cannot escape its two-sided karmic setup by using our free will to make choices that violate the principles that govern it. We need nothing more than to practice attuning ourselves to the ways that Christ, Krishna, and every other Self-realized master have revealed.

I sometimes think of this earthly life as a kind of TV game show. We can play it to win by following the lead of the blissful ones before us: the saints and sages of all religions. Or we can play it to suffer. The choice is entirely ours. God has become us. We are His children. He loves us, and He wants us to find our way back to Him. He is even willing to wait as long as it takes for us to get there. But the effort is ours to make. It's just a matter of using our free will to make the hero's journey: to choose the way of right action (*dharma*) and unconditional love.

IN PURSUIT OF DEVOTION

"No good end is ever reached without devotion" – Swami Kriyananda.

This makes perfect sense to me, and I trust you would also agree. Swami would often say that no true success is possible without involving the heart's feelings.

I would like to expand on that thought, but I must warn you at the outset: devotion is not my strongest suit. I've always been more of a "mental case" myself, so maybe these next few minutes will do us both some good.

I think of devotion as a language. When you grow up with a language, it becomes second nature to you. Without having to think about it, the words you use to express what's on your mind just come to you as you need them.

Devotion, however, is not a language that is widely spoken today in our Western culture. Far more common is the language of worldly ambition and material desire. That's the one we use for getting ahead, for getting what we want, and for getting around the idea that devotion is essential to our greater happiness.

Devotion to God is a language I am still learning. I cannot claim to be fully fluent or refined in its usage. Maybe that's because, when I was younger, I did not hang out with devotional people. They were okay by me, but not as cool or successful as I wanted to be. I was more devoted, if you will, to the trappings of outward appearance and winning the approval of others.

The source of this mindset was, of course, that friendly foe that is constantly wanting our attention, the tireless ego: "C'mon, man, let's go have some fun. Devotion is for people with limited interests. You've got five good senses. Let's go show 'em a good time."

Alas, devotion to God and to egoic values are not compatible pursuits.

Since coming to Ananda, a lot has changed for me. But devotion doesn't come with the snap of your fingers, even if you really want it. You have to work at it with an attitude of openness and surrender. In this regard, I have found great inspiration in the words to many of Swami's songs, and there is one in particular that speaks to me as an affirmation.

"Walk like a man, even though you walk alone.
Why court approval, once the road is known?

Let come who will, but if they all turn home,
The goal still awaits you. Go on alone."

There is nothing wrong with seeking to experience the pleasures of this world, but it does become a question of how often, to what extent, in what spirit, and at what cost to our inner life we allow these to define us.

Simplicity and moderation are the principles we strive to practice at Ananda, and the reason is this: When you have less to get in your way, that less becomes more of what matters: creativity, gratitude, compassion, love, forgiveness, peace of mind, and joy.

Everyone knows the downside of having too many desires. They drive us to distraction, which can make us a little crazy. But here's a tremendously encouraging fact: *We can change.* This is perhaps the most important asset in our bag of tricks, because unlike any other creature, we are not bound to our conditioning, no matter how deeply imprinted it may be. We can even develop devotion to God if we didn't have it before.

As Meister Eckhart said, the seed of God is in us. We don't need a full moon or the right alignment of stars to plant that seed in fertile soil; it was planted the day we were born. We just need to do some serious weeding so that its growth isn't choked off or stunted.

Weed out the fears. Weed out the anger, the old grudges and griefs, the disappointments. And then get out the watering can and give that seed some *prana*, some life force, to help it blossom forth and reach maturity.

There's another reason to nourish that seed, and it has to do with what happens if you don't. The universe, you see, has a slightly perverse sense of humor, and to the extent we resist making positive changes, it will hammer us with setbacks until those changes are made. Do you need more devotion in your life? The universe will let you know in countless little ways, and sometimes in big ways too.

Devotion is a feeling, but in part it is also a skill, and skills are acquired through practice. If you're a bit of a "mental case" too, practice chanting or *japa*. Repeat God's name or a sacred mantra until your exasperated brain just shuts itself off.

Practice living simply. Moderate your desires. Practice serving where service is needed with no ulterior motive or personal agenda. When we get away from "What's in it for me," we discover a freedom that no material advantage can match. And in that spirit, devotion grows deeper and stronger every day.

WHO IS A TRUE CHRISTIAN?

One of the characteristics I love about Yogananda's teachings is how every precept and principle is inseparable from every other. In our beginning Ananda meditation class, for example, we talk about the "eight aspects of God"— peace, calmness, wisdom, power, love, joy, sound and light—and how each of those qualities leads us naturally into the other seven. How can you have love without joy? Or peace without wisdom? Or the sound of Creation without the light of God?

The truths that Yogananda articulated are like the colors of a rainbow. Each one is distinct and yet indivisible from the others. They function as an integrated whole. You cannot extract the yellow or green from all the other colors. That's because there is fundamentally only one color, which is purely and simply clear. What we see in a rainbow are the ways that radiant light is refracted into the hues of our visible spectrum as it passes through the prism of sunlit raindrops.

Oneness—that kind of oneness—is a theme that runs through every facet of the lessons we are here to learn. The great saint Ramana Maharshi was once asked, "How should we treat others?" He answered simply, "There are no others."

But we forget, don't we, that we are all of that same clear light. Our oneness is hard to relate to, and furthermore most of us rather enjoy the thought that we are different. We like to think that we're special, a stand-alone color apart from the rest of the rainbow. We cultivate a personality, acquire habits and patterns of behavior, develop desires and opinions, ride on waves of emotion, and often fall into moods. In short, we are trained by the worldly lives we lead to turn our focus outward, under the expert direction of our social conditioning and our egoic tendencies.

When you have two individuals, each with his own accumulation of countless likes and dislikes, and then extrapolate to a planet of seven billion people swirling in a vast array of disparities and judgments, the result is the crazy and often dysfunctional world we have today: political parties, tribes, ethnicities, and nations engaged in degrees of disagreement and strife. Nowhere is this more evident than across the spectrum of religious dogmas and creeds, sometimes erupting into acts if war.

Christianity itself has splintered into many sectarian interpretations of what Jesus taught, into what Yogananda has called "churchianities." Most of those who adhere to a particular set of Christian creeds, whether Catholic, Baptist, Lutheran or any other, are apt to believe that their version is the one and only that Christ plainly intended. Other interpretations are rejected straightaway.

Yogananda came to the West to set the record straight, to bring back original Christianity, the true teachings of Christ. As he often said, Christ was crucified once, but his teachings have been crucified ever since.

When you get to the heart of the issue, it has nothing to do with organized religion of any sort. True Christianity is about right living. It's about the Golden Rule: doing unto others as you would have them do unto you. . . because there are no others. It's about making the effort to attune yourself to the study and practice of those eight aspects of God's divine consciousness.

Jesus put it in no uncertain terms: "Seek ye first the kingdom of God, and all these things shall be added unto you." He didn't mean we would then receive fame or fortune or anything else that is mortal by design. He meant that in devoting ourselves to finding and knowing God, we will attain what we really crave and cannot have in any other way: peace beyond the limits of our understanding; calmness so deep as to give us the strength to stand unshaken amid the crash of worlds; the wisdom of superconscious intuitive insight; the power of self-control; love without condition; joy that exceeds even our concept of happiness; the resounding experience of AUM in body, mind, and soul; and inner communion with the Light of the Lord.

What in this world compares with any of that? And yet we allow ourselves to favor all manner and description of lesser pursuits, assuring that we will experience some form of disappointment as our dreams and fleeting pleasures fade away.

Yogananda said that we begin to change when we finally tire of the "anguishing monotony" of falling into the traps of our worldly designs; when we turn within and seek our happiness in the heart of ourselves instead of out in the world; when we start to focus on giving instead of getting; when we aspire to become the true Christian that God sent Jesus to model for our salvation.

In this lifetime we of Ananda have been blessed with another extraordinary model to observe, study and emulate: Swami Kriyananda. I know of no one who faced more seemingly impossible challenges, who endured more physical illnesses and betrayals, and yet who rose above every obstacle and setback to accomplish astonishing successes in multiple fields of creativity and inspiration, all the while maintaining a state of blessed inner bliss. Isn't that what we want also?

The trouble is, we get sidetracked. We look outside ourselves for the answers and happiness we need to make us whole. Those who are true Christians—whether Hindus, Muslims, Buddhists, Jews, followers of Christ or any other Self-realized master—are those devoted to serving God without personal motive or expectation. It is they who also thereby serve all of humanity and their own highest potential at the same time. If there is a higher calling, I don't what it would be.

It is Swamiji again who showed us that self-offering is its own unrivaled reward. Nothing he ever did was about him. And nothing he ever accomplished or endured was able to interfere with the love and light he expressed. As he wrote in his song *In the Spirit*, "I was caught up in ecstasy. 'Twas a day sanctified by God. There He showed me the gifts of heaven, gifts that all seeking Him should know…"

It is tempting to excuse ourselves from that level of consciousness, to say that Swamiji was simply more advanced than any of us. Maybe so. But wouldn't we all like to have what he had: inner peace and joy? Wouldn't we like to know what it means to be eternally free? Nobody gets there by shrinking from the tests that come to us or by asking, "What's in it for me?"

As Master's unwavering disciple, Swamiji was ever the true Christian. He urged us to make the same commitment for one reason only: because it is the way to the goal of life, to *Satchidananda*. . . ever existing, ever conscious, ever new bliss. Returning to our home in God is a journey of ultimate simplicity. We think of it as complicated merely because it requires us to be courageous and strong, to let go of priorities that compete with our spiritual growth. We think of it as complicated because it means turning away from the peer pressures and conformities that bind us to society's false promises and delusions. When we are caught in that mindset, we are trying to win the unwinnable game.

Love, serve, and rest in God. Such is the way of the yogi, the true Christian in every respect.

CHAPTER 6

The Quest

"Hasten slowly and ye shall soon arrive."

Milarepa

REELING ON THE ROAD TO REDEMPTION

G rowing up Catholic, my only afterlife choices were Heaven or Hell. I knew how to wind up in Hell. Getting into Heaven would not be so easy.

It wasn't until I came to Ananda that I learned my actual destiny is freedom in God. It sounded too good to be true, but I was assured by Yogananda himself, in his writings and recorded talks, that someday, at the end of some incarnation, I would arrive at *Satchidananda*: ever existing, ever conscious, ever new Bliss. Good news doesn't get any better than that.

Then I reflected on how far from "there" I still am. It was deflating. The list of challenges before me was not a short one. Nor is it today. Earthly desires, attachments, habits, doubts, fears, and moods. . . the inventory takes up plenty of my mental and emotional space. This was the start of a conversation inside me that still continues. . . .

"Thank God I have gurus to show me the way.

"Too bad you don't listen to their advice more often!

"But to my credit, I no longer yearn for celebrity, fortune, or power. That should move me a rung or two up the ladder, wouldn't you think?

"Yes, but sensuality flaunts its wares on many of your favorite travel routes, and you find yourself taking notice. Thoughts of food, fantasy, fun, and romance are seldom far out of your mind.

"Am I strong enough to play at those roadside attractions and walk away unscathed?

"I'm afraid not. A good definition of delusion is believing that you can fool around in sensuality's quicksand without getting sucked in.

"Okay, but wait, there is more good news to speed my rescue if I should start to sink. I have learned Kriya Yoga, which promises to burn up seeds of my karma with every Kriya breath I take. Maybe I can play in the quicksand and offset its effect at the same time.

"That's the kind of reasoning that keeps adding karma to your tally even as you manage to shed other parts of it too. Surrender is in your name, but not so much in your nature.

"Hmmm. . . But isn't it true, as Christ said, that I have the power to become a Son of God, and that all I have to do is unlearn everything else that gets in the way? I'd say that's more good news. Although I've become complex, remembering how to be simple again should be simple. Right?

"Simple, yes. Easy, no. And if the truth be known, you are not ready to make the final push. That's because you don't really want to do what you have to do to win your way out of here yet. You think the unlearning should be more fun than it is, and that's why you often still look for it in outside pursuits. Since freedom in God is your destiny, you've been content to take your time about it."

Is it any wonder, with that sort of figuring and fussing, that we're so adept at talking ourselves into a muddled state? The problem, it seems, is that we are desperate to find some slack in the discipline required to ferry us across the ocean of delusion.

When I was in college, I majored in history. It's a fascinating field of study, very underrated in this era of specialized, high-tech concentration. What history has shown us is that we are often too smart for our own good. Despite our impressive mental capacity, we frequently misuse it, giving too little thought to the consequences of what we seek to accomplish.

You may have noticed that other animals do not have this problem. Complexity and delusion are not among the traits that typify the species below us on the cranial IQ chart. Poor creatures, they lack our analytical and creative faculties, and are forced to rely on instinct for everything they require. But you may also have noticed that, to their credit, they are not cursed with confusion, nor with the tangled webs we weave when our brainpower seduces us into thinking that we can get away with breaking the rules of the game. Animals live simply, entirely within their means, and entirely in the moment.

So, here we are at the top of our planet's food chain, able to reason and rationalize, able to invent and produce, and quite likely to convince ourselves that we are doing it all ourselves, under our own power. In a sense, this is true. We are free to choose, and thus free to sink or swim according to our mood and motivation. Unlike other animals, we can dwell in the past and plan far into the future. Living in the present isn't a necessity for us, it's an option.

But there's a downside to this precious gift of choice, especially when we overlook where its power comes from. Fear, worry, doubt, anger, envy, sorrow, and suffering are also among the items we are free to choose as the events of our lives unfold, and some of us are rather skilled at staying in close touch with these disorderly emotions.

Much of the trouble for us is that we've been socially trained to be insecure. And when you have a world of insecure people, pretending to know what they're doing, you have the world we live in today: an asylum of sorts that is run by the inmates.

Meister Eckhart, the great Christian mystic, said "I move my hand, and Christ moves who *is* my hand." Our divine union with Christ already exists. There is no separation except as we perceive and presume it to be.

Is it a difficult task to move beyond that sense of separation? Oh, yes, indeed. We're up against the tyranny of our own logic. We need to think out of the box that binds us to facts, figures, opinions, and dogma as the source of what we claim to know. Such information may not itself be harmful, but it obscures our oneness with God and the Infinite Christ Consciousness of which we are made.

The good news is, we're really almost there. It's just on the other side of where we are now.

I and Other

Life is a dance. You've heard that before. Every moment offers a new set of rhythms and flows to interpret. Sometimes the dancing is done with beauty and grace, and sometimes it is not. The question is, in this tango of the intertwined, who is the one who leads when the tune is called?

In the ballroom of human relationships, the pairing of the impulsive ego and its more conscientious partner, the super-ego, is always an interesting match. Attunement and mutual trust is required. This, however, is not achieved when the ego is determined to take control. Unfamiliar with when, why, and how to make all the right moves, it can quickly turn the tango into an ungainly tangle instead. As comic relief, this can be entertaining, but not in a way that serves the choreography or composition.

I have often been amazed at how many of us, myself included, still find it hard to surrender the floor, even to one who knows better. The little egoic self, it seems, would rather appear in command than allow another to steer who could skillfully lead the way. "Other," as opposed to "I," is often viewed as a threat to "my" self-existence and self-image.

"Other" and "I" are frequently at odds in matters of perception especially. At times, for instance, we have all been afraid of the dark, fearing that it was hiding something, an "other" that was out to get us. As children, in bed at night, we may have even imagined an "other dressed to kill." Fueled with adrenalin, our thoughts raced like stampeding horses, and turmoil churned inside us. Later, in the light, we saw what we could not see at the time—"other" in familiar attire" or "no other at all"—and we heaved a sigh of relief.

Now that we are much older, what we tend to fear most is a darkness more subtle and pervasive. In the shadows of our imagination, monsters of a different sort are apt to gather. We worry that we could lose what we treasure most, especially the ones we love, our mental abilities, and our physical health. Maybe we worry, too, that death will find us unprepared to meet it. In such a state of mind, we fail to see that instead of trying to *get us*, something or someone in this worldly experience is trying to *get us out!*

Ultimately, our dance of life needs to be led by the "Other" who can guide us to its final bow, the one who is our true partner in God. It is he, the Guru, in spirit and in truth, who is ready to guide us gracefully into the bliss of becoming the dance itself.

Truly, there is no darkness, no stumbling, and no fear when we can surrender fully to that Other's lead, when we make the attitudinal shift from egoic pre-occupation to Self-awareness.

A true story in a mere eleven sentences captures the essence of this lesson more eloquently than any treatise could. "This year began badly," wrote Sarah Hawk in her journal. "One day I woke up and started having seizures. They got worse and worse. It looked like a brain tumor, but it turned out to be epilepsy. Serious epilepsy. Now I am on medication for the rest of my life. It makes be clumsy. It makes me forget things. It makes me throw up."

Sarah slumped into a pall of self-pity. She stopped dancing altogether. And then in a single, Other-inspired epiphany, she turned the whole experience right side up. "Now I realize this was a great year. It was the year I didn't get a brain tumor." What Sarah got instead was a deeper love of life and all that it offers. With understanding and acceptance, she transformed her disease into the gift of a new, more expansive "I," and it took her to a place within her heart and soul that radiates peace and light.

Life is a dance. You've heard that before.

HELD BY THE HOLDING

Born to bear the burden of a human brain, I grapple with concepts that exceed the perimeter of mindful understanding. God, soul, AUM—all can be explained, but hardly do the explanations quench a thirst to *know* them. Books and oral teachings bring a measure of comprehension, and I can spout their content, combine them into writings and oral teachings of my own, and thus appear learned to myself and others. But only in a human manner of speaking. The *knowing* is not there.

Nearing the end of a blessed seclusion, reading again *The Essence of the Bhagavad Gita*—one of the most important books since the Bhagavad Gita itself— I am absolutely in awe of the consciousness and understanding of its authors: Paramhansa Yogananda and Swami Kriyananda. This is not a book composed of merely human intelligence. For anyone who wonders what life is about, the answer, both in utter simplicity and brilliant annotation, is superbly rendered in this channeled volume of wisdom.

The authors tell me here—as all saints and sages have emphasized elsewhere— that I have the God-given power to rise to their level too. And in my mind I believe it, just as I am equally aware that my willingness to "give it my all" has been missing in action. A jabbery, flattering voice in my head argues that spiritual reading, listening to inspiring lectures, living in spiritual community, and serving others as an Ananda minister, is really enough. Isn't it?

Well, I suppose we know the answer to that. My particular plane of achievement and comfort, no matter how it may compare to that of anyone else, has nothing to do with where it needs to be. What I want—the realization of God— has clearly been too much a part-time pursuit.

But I do believe I'm leaving my seclusion with a deeper sense of what it means to be accepting and calm. I can see that as each of my karmic tests has been notarized by Spirit, it is plainly a waste of life to deny, ignore, or resist it. In the past I was not swayed to this point of view. I frequently made it my self-righteous duty to counter-offend when faced with rudeness or irresponsibility; to hold others at fault for failing to meet my expectations; and generally to complain about slights to my personal agenda. My reactive desire, and sometimes my actual conduct, inclined toward evening the score.

It is easy to recognize now that karma replies to my actions, directly or indirectly, in every situation, and that my thoughts are not immune to its doings either, returning in kind what has been set in motion, like a circle completing itself.

I especially like a reference to karma by Ralph Waldo Emerson. Along with the Bhagavad Gita's words on the topic, this is what put me in mind of how nonacceptance only assures that history will repeat until its message is calmly received and absorbed. Emerson viewed the world as a simple, elegant equation which, "turn it how you will, balances itself. Every secret is told, every crime is punished, every virtue rewarded, every wrong redressed, in silence and certainty."

It's that "in silence and certainty" part, orchestrated beyond the reach of mind, that I was unwilling to fully trust. I wanted a role in meting out the justice that was due—just to make sure that God was not otherwise engaged when someone committed a misdemeanor against me—and needless to say, my way seldom had wisdom or a lasting effect to recommend it.

I look at our world today—the strife that infects personal affairs and international relations—and I see that human consciousness is stuck in the payback mentality that has characterized much of my own thinking. It scars the heart, scuttles the chance for solution, and fails to understand why. We are held by what we hold onto. I think it's just that simple.

IMAGINE THE POSSIBILITIES

Back in the early '70s, I was a huge fan of the comedy troupe known as Fire-sign Theater. Satirical, insightful, and very funny, those four guys pilloried our systems and behaviors across the entire spectrum of our social customs and beliefs. *Everything You Know Is Wrong* was one of their best record albums. Its title was right on the mark.

Yet, those pilloried systems and behaviors have hardly changed. Fresh names replace the old ones in the news as years go by, but the news itself stays much the same. With satellite technology, reports of our unlearned lessons simply arrive a lot faster.

One of those unlearned lessons is revealed in what and how we teach in our schools. To our enormous detriment, we are failing to deliver an educational experience that translates into happier, healthier children and adults, imbued with a level of consciousness that is sorely needed everywhere. We see today in the conduct of business and government, and also to a great extent in the arts, a self-indulgent bias that subverts the essential welfare of our planet and ourselves.

Thankfully, for those desiring a more effective learning experience, one that teaches abstract thinking in pursuit of real solutions to persistent problems, and that cultivates essential inner skills as well as career abilities, a brilliant alternative is at hand.

In today's educational landscape, Ananda's Living Wisdom Schools are unique, based on the concepts and curricula presented in Swami Kriyananda's book *Education for Life*. To understand why, it is helpful to look more closely at the reason so much of what we presume to know turns out to be false. The power of our social conditioning is a good place to start.

Living in today's Western culture, in particular under its daily assault of news, hype, and minutiae, it is no surprise that people lose sight of life's true purpose and meaning. Society's movers and shakers, claiming to know what is best for us—a Coke on a hot day, a luxury cruise when we need a break from the stress of a busy career, or a numbing pill for chronic depression or pain—are constantly trying to persuade us that happiness lies in external, materialistic answers to our problems.

Thus, we tend to find ourselves strapped to the seat of a rollercoaster car as it speeds up, down, and around on a ride that does not stop. Where is the meaning?

What we need is a whole new approach to living, learning, and being: organic, holistic, sustainable, and solution-minded. It has to be all-inclusive. And now that approach is in focus. Living Wisdom Schools at Ananda Village in the Sierra foothills, in Palo Alto, Portland and Seattle, and in Assisi, Italy, address the individual in body, mind, and soul. Graduates far exceed the general public in academics, social adjustment, confidence, poise, and creative expression.

If you are a parent, your child needs you to look at the difference that a Living Wisdom School can make in his or her life.

Chapter 7

Love

Nowhere have I been that serves me well except in love.
In love is the only where to be.

LOVE IS A KIND OF LITERACY

A beautiful Hasidic proverb states, "The community of the living is the carriage of the Lord." But what we see worldwide today is that carriage riddled with invectives and bullets. In too many places our precious global community lies in tatters. We can point to scores of reasons why—legacies of ethnic fears and hate, personal and national greed, religious madness, extreme patriotic allegiances—but it all comes down to the absence of love.

Who is at fault? *Who isn't?* We have grown up learning to view the pursuit of happiness as the ultimate competitive sport, and so we exclude or seek to neutralize others, thinking of them as impediments in our quest for the "good life" and its rewards. It goes against the grain of our social conditioning to believe that loving the disaffected is the way to greater happiness for all.

Two other quotes worth pondering are first from the poet Emily Dickinson, who wrote, "Who has not found the heaven below will fail of it above." And from Saint Bernard that "Love seeks no cause beyond itself and no fruit; it is its own fruit, its own enjoyment." But few are willing to trust in love except on a limited, self-serving scale, and so are unwilling to test if love is truly as Saint Bernard said. Instead, the vast majority competes for society's prizes, with each contestant losing the game of finding his heaven below, and failing of it above.

Love is a kind of literacy. When we are willing to put another's welfare ahead of our own, we are literate in love, and our relationships grow and deepen, able to survive and thrive even as problems intrude. To be illiterate in love is not to be bad, only ignorant of its value, and consequently at the mercy of whims and fragilities in affairs of the heart.

Love is also a consciousness, and loving is a learnable skill. It takes unwavering willingness, patience, forgiveness, and great effort to master the art of it, but he who has done so has found his "heaven below." Once in love, he is in it for ever more.

In the Bible is the story of the prodigal son. The lesson of it is most of all of the father, who rejoices at his son's return from a dissolute life, having never surrendered his love to judgment, anger, or regret. He celebrates the occasion with a welcome and a feast to the full extent of his wealth and jubilation.

To those who disappoint us, and who disappoint themselves; to those who would do us harm; and to those estranged of God and His ways, the only curative response is "Love them more."

Is this sure to be difficult? Oh yes, it will be at first the most difficult choice of all, but no other will begin to reinstate the community that is "the carriage of the Lord."

LOVE AT FIRST SIGHT

I have fallen in love three times within seconds of meeting the woman who stole my heart. Each of these relationships grew in depth of love during the years we spent together, and that depth has not diminished with separation. Gratefully, I have said to each of these three, "I have loved you for who you are, and for who I am when I'm with you. I have loved you for what you have made of yourself, and for what you have made of me."

Human love is a fascinating phenomenon that largely defies description except in general terms. That's because the love we feel for another—romantic, erotic, platonic, beguiling, or some combination of these—is always specific to the person who is under its spell. A measure of helplessness comes with it too. When love strikes, there is no getting around it. You are struck, stuck, and summarily swept away.

As an aside, it has always seemed humorous and odd to me that in Roman mythology, love is aroused when Cupid, a chubby little minor god who is hardly appealing himself, nor seemingly worthy to be the deity of desire, shoots his potion-tipped arrow into the body of his quarry. Wild behavior ensues that Shakespeare and others have portrayed with comic genius.

It is said that Cupid is boyish because human love is irrational and uncontrollable. Yet, also oddly enough, no one in this irrational, uncontrollable state ever complains about it! On the contrary, the reaction is almost universally giddy. We love to be in love, even though it often reduces us to a puree of our inner composure.

More than this cannot be explained, for human love is not formulaic. It does not try to make sense of itself. Like a force of stealth and surprise, it invades where it will without warning, and captures whom it chooses. Those who are carried away may try to tell you why, but they cannot, because love is greater than any bouquet of words that one can arrange to say how it feels, greater than any list of a lover's attributes and charms. Falling in love just happens, sometimes in a moment's meeting, sometimes slowly until the moment strikes.

Love at first sight is a hoot, and you simply have to love it.

START WHERE YOU ARE

How do we learn to love? and then learn to love more and more?

There is no secret approach, technique, tactic, or system to apply. We learn to love by loving. Wherever you are today, that's where you start. Does your ego have other plans? a self-indulgent activity, perhaps, or a grievance to file with folks who have stepped on your toes? Then now would be a perfect time to put those aims aside and find someone to serve.

Salmon swim upstream, against a powerful current, to lay their eggs. It's a sacrifice they make for the next generation, and though they are driven by instinct rather than individual choice, the act is one of love.

We, too, as we strive to increase our capacity to love, will often find the current of our conditioning to be a challenging force. Are we surprised? This is the planet of *dwaita*, where every positive trait is possessed of its negative dual. It takes courage and strength to buck the tide of unloving thoughts and behaviors, whether from dark energies or from within ourselves. Welcome to the way forward. It can be a tough one.

But love is like every virtue. The more of it you give, the better you feel. Think of it as a muscle that gets stronger the more it is exercised and toned. From our storybook days, we think of love as romantic, a smooth sail from first blush into the sunset. But much of what is required is to crew the vessel of love through the chopping seas and storms that are certain to test it.

Each of us is different in personality and the history that informs it. How can we expect that "happily ever after" will carry on of its own accord? Without assiduous effort, it may not survive the honeymoon!

It is not, however, such personal love that is so desperately needed. Greater is the love that enfolds in its arms the stranger, the outcast, the sorrowful, the abused. Can we learn to feel that love too? Even with commitment and energy, it is likely to come in a lifelong series of victories and setbacks. But every step that brings us closer together as a world family is a source of joy. When you need an incentive to learn to love more, there it is.

IN THE SWAY OF PERIL'S WAY

Do you love to shop? It's no wonder that so many people do. In this modern world of amazing gadgets and gismos, of got-to-have-it doodads and devices, our eyes are assaulted daily with alluring goods to have and to hold.

Shopping today is America's national pastime. Department stores, brand stores, and malls have become our culture's popular destinations for their feast of tempting consumables. In our collective consciousness, needing has been overrun by the habit of wanting. "Shop 'til you drop" is the motto of some, who wear it like a badge to be admired.

Fashion, too, is sold with enormous appeal, as if it were the Holy Grail of social acceptance. We have become a nation of fashion conformists. Although our choice of furnishings, outfits, and accessories may appear to us to be unique, the greater truth is that Madison Avenue tells us what is "in", and we choose from the choices it gives us. In total, its array of genres, colors, types, models, facsimiles, and styles is patently staggering, which enables the impression that we are not like everyone else.

Someone once noted humorously that fashion is that which "goes in one year and out the other," but that hardly deters a great many folks from climbing aboard the train to trendy persuasion. America's economic health is fed by and large by money spent as latest fashions prescribe.

Is this bad? Does it make us wrong?

In a deep sense, yes, it is and it does. That is not to say that a person who loves to shop is bad, but shopping just to shop, or to be on a constant lookout for the next impulsive purchase, is time spent without meaning or personal growth.

And worse, it is a misdirection of love. Energy and vitality flow out of us with every material desire we express. It is not surprising to observe that shoppers who shop to shop, spending their love like largesse in dreams or pursuit of unneeded possessions, often have less of it to give to others and to God.

Each of us likes what we like, and owning things of quality and utility is highly practical. The only question is, how often are those items put to use or properly enjoyed? Are they operated, handled, worn, driven, applied, maintained, and valued as their quality and utility would merit? Or do they live in closets, drawers, shelves, sheds, garages, or in plain sight, seldom remembered except as part of one's cache?

I do not exclude myself from wanting things that I do not need. Things of beauty, refinement, comfort, and convenience provide a source of pleasure that does no harm. For the sake of our love, however, it is crucial that we discriminate between having enough and too much. When simplicity crosses the line to excess, our spiritual vitality suffers the effect.

Temperance is love. Prudence is love. In cultivating them, our love expands, and with it a joy that acquisitions and fashion cannot match.

BEHOLD

Through our eyes, which are so small, yet the entire world appears and busily comes to life. It's amazing what the eyes take in. They behold for us the full ballet of our being, the dance of our years. Wondrous are they and what they see.

Yet, larger and even more wondrous is the heart, for when it is fully open, the invisible comes to life as well. The heart sees what the eyes overlook: the love of which the world is made, the love we are here to know and to share. Within the heart's gaze, divinely guided, is all creation beheld, beating of love.

———————

What are the rules that govern the ways of love? Alas, there appear to be many where none should ever be. Love is unconditional, or it is something else. Even to define it is to risk a limitation of its scope. Where love is true, it needs no stipulation, no governing code. Love breaks every rule that would enclose it.

In the story of Naresh and the saint who becomes his guru, the saint continues to ask him, "Who are you?" Not until Naresh, after years of reflection, is able to forego his self-definitions, is he able to give the one and only answer: "I know who I am, but there are no words with which to speak of it."

So it is with love. When the words of it finally fail and only its feeling remains, love is fully expressed.

———————

Sometimes good news and bad are so interwoven, it is hard to know which is which. Nothing is one or the other until we decide what to call it.

If a loved one is in great pain, and that pain is taken away, but the loved one is also taken away, is that good news or bad? Even in our sense of terrible loss, I believe we must say this is good, for love is always wanting the best for others.

⸻ ⸳⸳⸳ ⸻

Every fear is a fear of loss. One cannot truly love what he fears to lose, and only love can break the spell he is under. It takes a leap of faith which, when finally taken, does not disappoint.

⸻ ⸳⸳⸳ ⸻

To know that God is Love is to know the Law of Karma as its accomplice. Karma's sole purpose is to render loving guidance, to reveal what does and does not work. As often as it is misunderstood or sadly ignored altogether, it never seeks merely to punish, or to stray from its fundamental intent.

But what about the pain it causes? Some of it is severe, and not merely physical either. Where is the karmic love in tragic events, cruel disease, famine, poverty, homelessness, and the like?

We only experience pain when we are not ready to understand or accept the reason for it. Pain is nothing but a means of communication, meant to steer us to live with love instead of the choices that hurt us.

But some of what happens to people is plainly unfair and sometimes horrific. How are we to absorb as coming from love the killing of innocent victims in wars, fits of rage, and natural disasters?

Each of us has lived countless lives, in which we have played every role in the spectrum of human experience. We have "been and done it all." We have come to this incarnation with karmic debts yet to pay, otherwise our business here would be finished, and we would be as love itself, abiding in some higher realm. The cruelties we perceive are part of the karmic curriculum, aimed at correcting the cruelties we have caused. They persist until all corrections are made, until we and love are one. What comes of itself, let it come. Rather than label it good or bad, embrace it. Its purpose is deep. Do not dwell on the surface of its message. Read beneath the lines and see the love.

Human love, like any adventure, is not a safe experience. It cracks you wide open, exposing you to every vulnerability you possess. Does love make you afraid of what you might lose? Beloveds die, just as you will die. Love does not always feel good.

Surrender to love, and you strip yourself naked before it. Nothing is withheld, least of all your doubts and fears. At times it will be inconvenient or out of control. But if it is true, your heart will make it right. That's because love is not about him or her, it's about you; about what you are willing to give and give up. What you seek will circle around to you.

Human love is not safe. No lesson ever is until you embrace it all the way.

CHAPTER 8

Death and Dying

"Thou shalt understand that it is a science most profitable,

and passing all other sciences, for to learn to die."

Heinrich Suso

WHAT COMES AROUND

Does talk of death make you a little uneasy? Most people look for ways to change the subject.

It seems that in every culture, death is the source of superstitious behaviors and carefully arranged rituals that we practice to ward it off. Trying to deny the seed of death within us is another way of attempting to avoid it, as if thinking that what we don't think about will somehow not affect us. Many of us prefer to make-believe.

Everyone since childhood has been aware of death, but as long as we're alive, death is that which happens only to others. We tend to ignore its presence until, in failing health, we end up cramming for peace of mind just as we crammed for exams in our school days.

What are we afraid of, a sudden plunge into the vast unknown? No doubt about it.

Death, as pictured from here, is the ultimate foreign soil, driving us to xenophobic extremes. Having no snapshots of its terrain to attract us, we incline to presume its features are stark and severe. As a place to refresh, it's a tough sell.

Death is entered in nakedness, alone. We are swept into its realm, unsupported by the props that reinforce who we think we are: our families and friends, our collected things, our resumes, our names. Death reminds us abruptly that we are not, and never were, the portraits of ourselves that we project.

This game we play is strange, to say the least. Although imagination is one of our celebrated strengths, we use it mainly to practice self-entrapment, inventing ways to snag ourselves on hooks of worldly obsession. Catering to our anxieties, we press for material comforts, financial cushions, career titles, and countless other ego-driven rewards.

What could be less prudent? Comfort and ease invite the very attachments that extend our delusions. They prevent us from dealing with why we are here and in what condition of spirit we will depart. By trying to escape or numb the tribulations of our lives, we do nothing to reduce the number of karmic encounters that yet await us, encounters that must be met and resolved before any meaningful comfort can occur.

Looking back on my years, I am struck by the amount of time I've devoted to devotionless living. With social ladders to climb and territories to claim, I was quick to postpone the care and feeding I needed more than these. Even now the neon lure of egocentric pursuits is sometimes stronger than my power to resist. The truth is, as Kriyananda would remind us, spiritual sincerity is not a door that one can easily open when, in this earthly house of mirrors, he remains in the trance of its reflection.

Ascended masters have counseled us that patience is the shortest route to God. In hearing this advice, however, we seem to interpret patience as procrastination. Not that we are inactive. Quite the opposite. But instead of using these precious years to probe and embrace the inner, eternal wonders of our being, we mostly spend them chasing visions of permanence which ever and again dissolve. Putting off the practice of connecting to God, we race for mortal gains. Until, that is, we perceive that our days are few. Until anxiously cramming for our final exam.

> *I hold in my hand the everywhere neverlasting.*
> *I see in my head the dance of changing forms.*
> *Now is what there is,*
> *And then it is gone.*
> *Now is what there is,*
> *And then I am gone.*

Maybe we are doing the best we can. Lots of false ideals and misguided perceptions are stacked against us. There is much of our learning to unlearn. Many of us, to some degree, are like the great comedian W.C. Fields, who discounted any belief in a higher purpose of life. During his last days, confined to a hospital room, Fields was visited by a friend, who was shocked to find him at a table, reading the Bible. "Bill, what are you doing?" the incredulous friend inquired. Fields replied in his famous, drawn-out manner of speech, "Looking for loopholes!"

Isn't that, in a way, a bit like most of us too? We look for avenues of escape from the karmic law of cause and effect. But the buck stops at mortality's last hurrah.

The trouble is, it is death instead of desire that people dread. We fail to see the connection, that dying is mostly a function of dying for more. To want is soon to need, and as need demands, one devolves from free spirit to slave. We long to be happy, yet so many of our emotions, beliefs and behaviors lead us astray of the goal.

The Tibetan Book of Living and Dying condenses our plight into a single sentence: "We need to make a very clear distinction between what is our *ego's self-interest* and what is our *ultimate* interest; it is from mistaking one for the other that all our suffering comes." Suffering has no objective existence, the author explains. It is only our aversion to it that causes it to arise. It is we who give it power. It is we, by our fears and contractive logic, who attract to ourselves the hardships that besiege us.

Thankfully, though, after lifetimes of getting it wrong, we start to get it right. We begin to look inward for answers to the meaning of life and death, and as we do, we redeem death of its dark disguise, discovering that its purpose is to show us how to live. The peace we long for comes from letting go of our worldly attachments. That is the lesson of death, and we don't have to wait to die to gain its reward.

Jesus, in the Gospel of St. Matthew, said: "He that findeth his life shall lose it, and he that loseth his life for my sake shall find it." In today's language: He who persists in his ego's self-interest is destined to remain in delusion, losing the chance to move beyond its material limitations. Delusion dissipates only as one overcomes the pull of such desires, breaking away from his tether to selfish pursuits. Then does he reap the ultimate freedom of divine reunion with God.

In the ending lines of his beautiful prayer-poem, St. Francis of Assisi takes us back to the truths we tend to forget. He beseeches his Lord to "make me an instrument of Thy peace," concluding:

> *For it is in the giving that we receive;*
> *It is in the pardoning that we are pardoned;*
> *And it is in the dying that we are born to eternal life.*

What are we afraid of, a sudden plunge into the vast unknown? Not if we get to know it while we are here.

Like a River in the Desert of Time

In today's competitive America, money is the mouse that roars. We have even been sold on its power to secure the future. Never mind the transparent myth that supports this misconception, it tones like a mantra in every commercial setting we encounter. Is it any surprise that principle and faith tend to suffer greatly at the altar of financial gain?

Consistent with money's preeminent place in society, making more of it is often a person's first order of business. Gotta get that raise! To many, this is their validation of worth, not to mention the means to exercise more expensive desires. But at the end of the day, what are we left with? Little by little, we ravage ourselves to earn those extra dollars, to win the next promotion, to get ahead of everyone we can.

Yet, the highest potential raise of all is the one we pray to forestall. Thanks to our conditioning and its skewed priorities, leaving this physical life tops the list of what we dread. Someday you and I will be lifted from this burden of flesh into the lightness of being, and we fear the event like a terrible curse. Death, poor fellow, has been cast in black to play the villain's role, his merciful nature despised. How easily a truth is inverted to serve a material wish, an emotional attachment, a selective blindness!

"Life is a vagrant," said Paramhansa Yogananda, "appearing and disappearing like a river in the desert of time." We cannot suspend its passage to suit our personal dreams. But damned if we don't make the effort for as long as breath allows. Why are we bent on regarding death as a loss? To the wise, there is no end as we perceive it. Death, for even the weakest and most profane, is a ticket to understanding beyond all earthly scope. Furthermore, for those who strive to put love ahead of material possibilities, death is a liberation from limiting dreams altogether.

In Shakespeare's *Measure for Measure*, with rapier-tipped irony, the Duke rails in earnest at the craziness of our ways: "Merely, thou art death's fool, for him thou labor'st by thy flight to shun, and runn'st toward him still. Happy thou art not, for what thou hast not, still thou strivest to get, and what thou hast forget'st. . . If thou art rich, thou'rt poor, for, like an ass whose back with ingots bows, thou bearest thy heavy riches but a journey, and death unloads thee. . . Yet death we fear, that makes these odds all even."

Is it by reason that we relegate life to a test of worrisome choices? Consider the tormented Hamlet, another Shakespeare character, as he agonized over avenging his father's murder. "To be, or not to be?" he weighed in anguish. But misreading between the lines, as we incline to do also, he set in motion more misery than he resolved. Hamlet, for all his nobility, was nonetheless contractive in both his logic and his actions from the outset. "To be, or not to be, *expansive. That* is the question" that Hamlet, in his reasoning, overlooked. To have answered in the affirmative would have spared him his tortured state.

The expansive heart transcends the temptations of clever worldly schemes. Its healing tonic is greater than any other, for it knows all experience of life, and especially that of death, as Divine expression.

I know that truth is often hard to swallow, mainly because we invest so much in the lies that would overturn it. Hooked on sensory feedback and its implied advice, we expect the truth to confirm what we see as real, though seldom is it the same for two observers. Unable to see with our eyes, for example, that matter is just an illusion, that in truth it is energy—perhaps even thought—slowed in its vibration to a visible, solid state, we claim to *know* what is only true within our window of sight. Beyond this narrow perspective—beyond the spectrum of light that stretches from infra-red to ultra-violet—truth expands to distant horizons that intuition alone is able to access.

Thus, by our bias for evidentiary proof, we cling to fractions and facets of truth as if they were complete. The result, in all of its myriad manifestations, is the evocation of pain.

Distortion, distraction, and disinformation—the "3 Ds" of self-created suffering—are in large measure the bases of our behavior, from which fear of death has ascended to the seat of control. Believing we can appease this fear by acquiring status and wealth, we perpetuate its reign.

One of my favorite aphorisms is appropriate to this discussion: "The first rule when finding yourself in a hole is to stop digging." But few look up from their busy shoveling to see wherein they stand. Thus, as another saying goes: "Getting older is a function of time, getting wiser is a function of will, and only the former is assured."

Wisdom begins with insight, not merely a recitation of popular doctrine. In his book *Rays of the One Light*, commentaries on the Bible and Bhagavad Gita, Swami Kriyananda opens each essay with these deeply meaningful words: "Truth is one and eternal. Realize oneness with it in your deathless Self, within." That is to say, truth emanates from experience, *inner* experience. "Within" is the one and only path to clarity that endures, the path of saints, for it far surpasses in verity the intelligence we claim from all external sources. It is by introspection and meditation that truth is *truly* discovered, that wisdom *truly* accrues. Fame and fortune for personal gain are as useful to the journey as a pair of cement shoes.

In moments of calm reflection, I try to look at it this way: I started out with nothing, I still have most of it, and when I take my leave of this plane, nothing will be there with me. What could be better? But calm reflection, alas, is not my unswerving response to the world around me.

I cannot fathom why we believe as we do, and why we behave as if opposing the qualities that would redeem us. I only know that I, too, am plagued with nagging resistance to counsel that puts my soul ahead of earthly satisfaction. Ego and its demands can be insanely compelling.

In a two-line poem by Robert Frost, our self-imposed condition is superbly juxtaposed to the nature of God:

> We dance around in a ring and suppose,
> But Secret sits in the middle and knows.

Here is the ultimate truth, eloquently stated. Its cosmic "middle" of knowing is the universe of the deathless Self, within. Money cannot secure it. Mortality cannot change it.

Even more succinct in explaining the nature of this one overarching verity, and thus the mind of the Infinite, is Yogananda's description: "Center everywhere, circumference nowhere."

For the devotee in search of this perspective, energetic inner daring is essential. Bringing it home to nest is a full-time occupation, for any true principle is not necessarily as the ego would like it to be, nor as we try to make it. First, last, and always, it is as it is. And sooner or later, just as death has the final word on this physical plane, God's truth has the final word in the Great Beyond.

⸻

As long as we are alive, death is within us. Few subjects, if any, are as thought about, talked about, written about, fretted about, and feared. Yet, in the end, all that is said of death is reducible to three words: **It's what happens.**

⸻

In Search of Transcendence

Years ago, when TV entertainment was cutting its teeth, *People Are Funny* was the name of a popular show. Gentle in its humor, it steered wide of today's aggressive themes and confrontational formats. But the show was always good for laughs as it recorded, in a sense, our convoluted thinking and antic behaviors.

Are we any less laughable now? Have our technological gains made us more socially advanced, more self-aware? Consider that one of our funniest routines continues to be the effort we make to bleach our thoughts of dying. It is almost a cultural imperative. Who are we kidding?

Dealing with death is perhaps the most difficult test that life presents. At least that's how most of us view it. Sure, we know that no one leaves here alive. But rare is the person who readies his heart and mind to make the crossing.

One of Buddhism's leading masters, Sogyal Rinpoche, suggests that we are afraid of death because we do not know who we truly are. "We believe in a personal, unique, and separate identity," he writes, whose existence "depends on an endless collection of things to prop it up." Because of this, in our late years especially, we often succumb to a kind of bewildering despair.

Ignoring the certainty of death until it is near, we tend to hide from ourselves, filling our time with tedious and trivial pursuits, mainly to keep from meeting the stranger inside us. Then, as the end approaches, collapsing our shelter of cards, we find ourselves in the harsh, accusing glare of our misspent years, chasing the glitter of fool's gold.

Oddly enough, we spare little time or thought for living either. My own father, like many of his generation, worked at his occupation until he retired, only to wind up lost in the land of not knowing what to do. Despite his contributions to the health and healing of his patients, and his material gains therefrom, the future he envisioned for himself was empty of meaning or joy. Worse, he feared the *real* future that awaited at the end of his days.

I have no doubt that my father's abiding desire was to live happily and well. But he was stopped cold, failing to embrace the life that his death would bring.

He, perhaps like most, invested the coin of his happiness in a dream of limited span, while before him lay eternity, seldom regarded.

We are here, and soon we are gone. "Reap the most you can of immortality," urged Paramhansa Yogananda. But who does? Rather, like dupes in a con game of our own egocentric device, dressed in our underwear like Hans Christian Anderson's ridiculous emperor, we hold that by our vaunted human intelligence, we are as finely and fully clothed as could be. Thus, our lives appear to be locked in re-runs of the past.

To befriend one's death while alive is to realize the mercy of its mission. Death is not the grim reaper of lore. It is, above all, a chance to wipe clean the slate of mistaken turns. And the beauty of it is, we don't have to wait to breathe our last to gain its worth. As we give ourselves fully to each moment in time, we realize without fear or regret, that "what is born will die, what is gathered will be dispersed, and what has been high will be brought low." These words of the Buddha are clear and correct, yet we act as if we could override them. People are funny, no?

On a subtler level, death delivers another lesson, too. This is not the place, it says, to lazily drift along. "Whatever we have done with our lives makes us what we are when we die," writes Sogyal Rinpoche, "*and absolutely everything counts.*" Inwardly, I suspect, we know this to be true, which may explain why death is feared so widely.

To reverse the habit of our worldly ways is a challenge more daunting in its demands—and more essential in its purpose—than any other we face. And if this were not hard enough, society's enormous momentum, driven by relentless pressure and propaganda to conform to its ways, is squarely pitted against us. Repeatedly we miss the mark, returning to try again as the elevator to Heaven's gate opens to a lower floor. Like the Bill Murray character in *Groundhog Day*, none of us gets out of this movie for good until we pass the exam of selfless love.

So, where do we start? How do we dump the notion that letting go of ego is losing the rich romance of being human? To reunite with our higher aim requires a journey of spirit beyond all socialization. Do you think you can make the journey on your own? If so, your pride will surely drive you to fail. Burdened as we are with worldly desires and habits, we can hardly expect to stay the course of a spiritual transformation without an expert guide: a guru, that is; one who has made the journey himself; a master who can demonstrate that life on earth is an "obstacle illusion," and lead the way through it to the soul's liberation.

Finding such a guide is not a casual task. Forget about running a Personals ad. A formal education will not help you either, nor even rigorous logic. To paraphrase an old cliché, when the pilgrim is ready, the avatar will appear. Getting ready is all about cutting loose of mortal ties.

On the subject of dying, a master is certain to emphasize a perspective beyond the norm: that preparing for death—one's final exam—is the most important "to-do" on anyone's list; that discerning the body's in-born illusory nature is critical to rising above its limitations; that the process of dying, when viewed from increasing earthly detachment, allows the ever expanding dawn of soul-knowledge. In surrender to the guru's wisdom and will—through attunement in particular—we reconnect with the consciousness that is our divine nature, dispelling our fear of death and replacing it with blessings of inner peace.

Thinking and writing about this is the easy part, of course. Living it is another matter. I, like most, have a long history of steeping in delusion's brew. But at least now I "get it," and more and more I am letting my guru lead me. Death is wearing a friendlier face these days.

WILLINGNESS AND FAITH

Nature is a fountain of boundless inspiration. Every plant, every creature, offers a message that speaks to us directly. As we tune into its wonders, we understand more of ourselves.

Consider the lowly caterpillar as it transforms into a butterfly. Is there a more miraculous image of relevance to our own lives? The caterpillar goes within, secluded in its cocoon from outward distraction. It reduces itself to the core of its being, aided and guided by an unseen, benevolent power. It literally dies to its former self, and then reemerges, a vision of winged beauty, free of its heaviness, no longer bound to the earth.

The memo in this for us is unmistakable. We, too, can remake ourselves simply by going within, and by doing the work that will break us free of the heaviness that is our ignorance. In surrendering ourselves to the process, we also attract that same invisible support, and when our transformation is complete, we find ourselves newly minted, able to soar at will with wings of inner joy above the mundane matters of this world.

The caterpillar operates on instinct. It is programmed by an automatic willingness and faith to rise from its limitations to a higher experience of life. These two qualities, willingness and faith, are essential to our progress also, but we do not have them instinctively or automatically at our command. We have to acquire and exercise them with will power and effort. Let's have a look at what this entails.

Everyone knows what it means to be willing. But faith is not so easily understood. Is it more than a belief? Yes, it is. Faith is born of *experience*. You have it because it has come to you as knowledge that is more than an external transfer of information.

Belief, on the other hand, is born of a personal desire, an empirical arrangement of facts, or someone's mere opinion. I can believe that global warming is a myth, or that justice will be served if my candidate is elected. I can even believe the earth is flat. But my experience of those beliefs is not likely to resonate with reality.

Nonetheless, good things begin with someone believing in their potential value. Problems arise only because this is a tricky planet. God has designed the game so that every positive external force or achievement is also possessed of its opposite. A coin has two sides; it cannot have only one. A pendulum swings to and fro; like it or not, fro gets equal time. A scientist harnesses the atom, turning its activity into useful energy for all, then someone else turns it into a bomb. Two opposing sides of the same capability.

The singer Dean Martin was once asked, "What do you believe?" He thought for a moment and then replied, "I believe I'll have another drink." It's a funny line, but hardly a conviction on which to build a purposeful or gratifying life. Sadly, we see that most people are *unwilling* to reach for more than a temporary fix to the problems that cause them to suffer. Looking outside themselves for answers, they are blind to the emptiness they continue to attract.

Belief becomes faith when it consistently gives us the experience of what we believed it would. I have faith in the force of gravity. For as long as I can remember, it has kept me from flying off into space. So far so good. I *believe*, however, that God could suspend the force of gravity at any given moment, and if He ever does, I will have to rethink my faith. Thankfully in the meantime, however, I can plan my days according to the high probability that I will remain in fundamental contact with the earth.

Faith of a spiritual nature is the power to draw to ourselves—to know and experience—the truth of who we are. We are divine immortals, eternally more than the bodies, brains, and obvious limitations we inhabit as human beings. As it says in our Ananda Festival of Light, after eons of time and repeated flights into darkness, we finally begin to ask, "Who are we in reality? For what end were we made?" We begin to seek the answers and the guidance that will lead us to faith in God and our eventual redemption.

But meanwhile, thanks to our social conditioning, we have plenty of hurdles to put behind us first: our stubborn habits, worldly ambitions and attachments, moods and material desires. The only thing more exhausting than striving for spiritual freedom is failing to make the effort, which guarantees another return to the wheel of karma and reincarnation without having made any significant progress. It is humorously suggested that when a newborn child draws its first breath and cries out loud, it's because it has suddenly recognized that "Oh, no, I am back here again!"

Great masters who come to us as gurus have all the tools, teachings, and techniques we need to gain enlightenment and liberation. They have been where we are, and they know the way out. Our task is simply to put what they offer as guidance into practice: self-study, self-control, sadhana, service to others, and satsang with like-minded souls. Of these is our destiny fulfilled: freedom in God and bliss everlasting.

In the seven months from August, 2015, to March, 2016, I had the privilege of watching as someone dear to me took willingness and faith to an extraordinary level of spiritual attainment. Tushti, my wife of 35 years, was diagnosed with cancer, and by the time we learned of this, the cancer was stage 4 and metastatic. Although her death was not sudden, it was a great loss to me and to everyone whose life she touched. Yet, her passing was also a very profound, instructive, and inspiring experience for reasons that speak directly to this discussion.

As a writer, it was my nature to record many of my thoughts during the time of Tushti's illness. In sharing some of them here, it is with the hope that each of us may better understand what death and dying is all about; and further, that we find ourselves able, as Tushti was, to come to the end of life with a trusting heart, an open mind, and a soul that has been purified of most if not all of the karma that binds us to the vagaries of a worldly existence.

What I gained in the course of this intimate process was my own faith in the promise of what lies ahead when we face our final exam with courage instead of remorse or despair, and with love instead of fear as we pass through the veil that separates this earthly life from the next one.

Tushti was about the last person you might suspect of developing a terminal disease. She had almost boundless energy, practiced yoga devotedly, ate a healthy diet, and was only 68 years old. **Lesson no. 1: We never know what God's plan for us might be.** It is crucial to be willing to face whatever hardship comes your way, because you can bet it has your name on it, and that it has come for a purpose. Every challenge we encounter is a chance to lay to rest an emotional, psychological, or spiritual limitation.

Tushti's condition was painful and terribly debilitating. She battled against it as best she could, but she also accepted that here was an opportunity to overcome any resistance to the message God was sending her: to deepen her attunement to Spirit. Tushti never lost the light in her eyes, her concern for the welfare of others, her innate kindness and sweet disposition, her appreciation for all that was being done for her, and her inner peace. She didn't want to die, but she wasn't afraid, and when it became obvious that her soul was trying to find its way out of her body, she gracefully allowed it to take its leave.

Lesson no. 2: When the outcome has been clearly ordained, let go and let God. No regrets. No complaints. Just willingness and faith.

In the last weeks of her life, it seemed almost impossible that she was still with us. A heartbeat and her breath were just about all that remained. Those of us at her bedside could only imagine that she had been given an extra-credit assignment as part of her final exam, that God was keeping her in that body long past its expiration date, whispering to her to show us that "This is how you do it." This is how you come to the end of your life, your heart filled with gratitude and love, no matter the pain and discomfort.

Lesson no. 3: We are here to offer ourselves in service and devotion to God and to each other for as long as we can, in whatever way we are asked. Tushti was serving us all right to the end, and from her we learned what it means to die with faith and willingness. I have never known a time that I cherish as much as those seven months we had together, and with those who so lovingly supported us.

Yet, several days after her passing, I was struck by the physical finality of her absence. What had been would be no more, and I wrote this reflection: "For thirty-five years I would hold my wife in my arms, feeling her breath on my neck. Today I held her in a carry-sack, containing two canisters of her ashes."

That was quite a moment for me. I will never forget it. **Lesson no. 4: In time this flesh, and all the features we identify as you and me, are reduced to about six pounds, a weight that will also later vanish into myriad other forms and expressions of the Infinite.**

Life goes on as we know it, and then life goes away. Or does it? The consciousness that we are is forever. In Swami Kriyananda's magnificent oratorio, Jesus on the cross sings these most poignant and reassuring words: "Birth, life, and death are one: veils of Thy love." They're just veils that we can part with dedicated attunement to God's ever present love, with willingness and faith.

Life goes on, and so do we, because death is merely a doorway to life continuing elsewhere.

Tragic events occur at times from far out of the blue, destined to turn our lives upside down or extinguish them altogether. Natural disasters and the ones we create ourselves are features of the landscape into which we are born. Who can know exactly why?

We tend to think of karma as a personal matter, but it can be collective as well. Nations and tribes accumulate karma, as do smaller and even seemingly random groupings of people. Members of these collectives are seldom conscious of the karmic connections they share. Perhaps the ties are other lifetimes old, and in view of this, we wonder: Was there a karmic relationship, for example, that encompassed all 230,000 people who were swept away on Christmas Eve by the massive Indian Ocean tsunami of 2004?

For the answer to questions such as this, I look to the East: to the ancient wisdom of avatars and sages; and to the light that shines in the East of a deep meditation. But sometimes, nonetheless, we are left with mysteries we cannot fully solve. Just as a cup cannot hold the contents of a much larger vessel, we cannot know if or how our past-lives connections may be at play in this one. The volume in the vessel that contains them is greater than that of our capacity to receive it.

Still, the message delivered in sudden misfortune is ever the same: Be ready to accept with equanimity all possibilities. Bad things happen to good and bad people alike. So, what is the good of denial, anger, or regret? What is the point of wishfully dwelling on a different outcome that did not occur instead? Help where you can. Pray to heal where it hurts. Feel, but do not lose yourself in emotion.

Calmness in time of sorrow or crisis is not easily won. We have been conditioned to worry and fear, to react and blame, to believe that suffering is cleansing. Truly, we have much to unlearn, and it is this reverse learning process that is the essential learning curve before us.

CHAPTER 9

Mind Games

"Mind is consciousness which has put on limitations. Once you were unlimited and perfect. Later you took on limitations and became the mind."

Ramana Maharshi

THE TREE AND THE ANGEL

A re you in your body-mind, or is it in you?

This is not a trick question, but the right answer is not the one that most people choose.

Quite understandably, we are raised to believe in the physical reality that surrounds us, and our senses support that belief every minute of the day. In agreeing with what they report to us, we experience separation. Objects appear at different locations in space, and time is required to move from one to another. You are there, I am here, and between us is a certain distance that is populated with other people and things. Quite understandable.

But just as the body-mind is an object too, there has to be a witness that observes it. Who, or what, could that be?

Wanting to know the answer, you decide to go looking for the witness. But right away you run into a problem. The witness is subjective. There is no "thingness" to find, and the body-mind cannot distinguish whatever is not objective. You've been stopped by a non-experience.

Despite this setback, you cling to your sense of "I am." It feels like an identity that is not yet fully rendered. As you start to weigh where to go with that, the ego in you is ready to make a play for it. "I am the body-mind," it asserts, "Trust me, and I will lead you to 'the good life.'"

For countless incarnations, the ego and you, as the body-mind, embark on worldly adventures that never entirely satisfy your relentless search for contentment. Alas, on each expedition, misery is a frequent companion too.

Once again, you remember the unfettered witness. Looking around, you feel that you have been hypnotized to accept a limited reality that is not having the happy effect you were seeking.

What can you do? How can you change that perspective to one that will serve you better?

Suddenly, you recall an image from your childhood. You were given the picture of a tree and told that an angel was hiding somewhere inside it. At first you saw only the tree, but finally you found the angel. Her face appeared in the leaves like a secret revealed. The angel had been there all along, merely hidden from ordinary vision.

An idea begins to dawn in you. The angel is like the witness, watching and awaiting discovery. She is your hidden nature, the consciousness at the core of your being. Tree and angel, body-mind and witness, become detectable.

In truth, you have never been your body-mind except as a series of sensory perceptions; except as you have been trained by your parents, teachers, and friends to agree; except as a false bundle of self-definitions. Your body-mind is in you.

Once you have seen the angel in the tree, your whole world looks different; and seeing yourself as the witness, as pure awareness, is tantamount to a revolution of infinite possibilities.

Does this mean you are not an actual person? In the dream of this physical reality, which is God's dream, of course you are a person. You cannot *undream* the awareness of that. It is the image of the tree without the angel. But you have seen the angel.

This entire point of view is an invitation. It's a calling to a new and higher experience of truth, knowledge, and happiness. It's an offer to enter the realm of the Self, where all becomes transparent, where the temporal is rendered eternal. All that is needed to enter that realm is to let go the branch of the tree that connects us to our body-mind identity.

Oh, but we keep hanging on, do we not? Letting go seems scary. We yet have attachments and unresolved fears that are deeply rooted in the dream. The drop seems a long way down.

But hope has risen above the horizon as well, for we have seen the angel, and we are beginning to know who we truly are. As our confidence increases, we learn to question our beliefs, and to question our former acceptance of a limited consciousness. We learn that we can tolerate the ego without giving it our attention, and that we can die to the notion that we are anything but divine. Our awareness is inexpressible, but we are its eternal gift.

<hr>

A CONVERSATION WITH MYSELF

"I am nothing," I reflected as I gazed overhead at the starry night. "My size and place in the vastness of billions of galaxies is too trifling even to be called absurdly trifling. Soon this 'I' will shed its visible disguise once again, and the dust of me that is left will disappear into gases, metals, flavors of ice cream, rabbits in hats, and a limitless number of other fleeting forms.

"Maybe so," an unseen voice replied. "Gone from here is gone, as you surmise, at least in any lasting material sense. But you're a stunningly powerful nothing nonetheless.

"What do you mean?"

"Consider the whole of the universe. From your point of view, it is inconceivably immense and still racing outward at the speed of light. But despite all of that, the universe is a single quantum system, and you have much to do with how it behaves. What do you think will happen when you, the observer-participant, are no longer present to affect its linear motion? Let me tell you, its motion will lose its linear appearance. After you leave here, hopefully for a higher dimension, the universe will cease to change or evolve. It will be without time, because you will not be here to move it along."

"That's ridiculous," I said.

"No, it's not," the voice insisted. "You are the one who is dreaming it into being, and you are at the center of how it unfolds. Others are doing the same, and they, like you, are at the center of their own universe-dreams. Your dream and that of everyone else—billions of them transecting into a mesh that is ever and never the same—is what the quantum is. It's a universe of dreamed up agreements, sustained by perceptions that are truly the stuff of nothing. When you exit from here to a higher plane, your vision will greatly improve, and you will see beyond the limits of your sensory perspective, into a timeless dimension that is where you are now without knowing it. Meanwhile, have a good time!

Thinking Out Of The Box

In several of his books, Swami Kriyananda refers to the Frenchman Rene Descartes, who is justifiably regarded as a true genius, primarily in the field of mathematics. Descartes is the father of analytical geometry, and by virtue of his studies of the human mind also, and its logical objectives, he is the one most responsible for the advent of the Age of Reason in the mid-17th century.

Descartes was an energetic and prodigious thinker, and also a man of God. He relied little on conventional thought in arriving at his discoveries, and more on his own intuition, investigation, and experience. Yet, of all that he achieved, we remember him first and foremost for a three-word statement: "Cogito ergo sum." The English translation takes five words: "I think, therefore I am." To this day that declaration is famous and firmly established in modern philosophy.

I can just imagine other scientists and philosophers of his era, upon reading Descartes' claim when it was first published, enviously saying, "Wow, I wish I had thought of that." At first blush it seems so perfectly cogent and correct. But the question that Kriyananda dared to ask is simply this: Is the statement true? Does it lead us to an understanding of the "am" that is I and you?

This raises another question too. Although we've been given the ability to think, can we ever know God by means of it, even at the level of genius? And the answer, to our frustration, is an unequivocal no. Thinking is an extremely useful skill in countless situations, yet it turns out to be a loser when it comes to the most important task of all: the experience of God-consciousness, leading us to reunite with Him in communion.

Descartes' declaration is not entirely wrong, but it has another leap to make before it can be understood as fully correct. There is an element missing in his conclusion. When we say "I think," where does that "I think" come from? What is the *source* (i.e. the Source) of that which tells me I am?

Is it the brain? Could this marvelous processing unit that resides between our ears also be the origin of what comes through it? Sorry, but no. The human brain is an awesome receiver and repository of information, but despite its stupendous computing and reporting prowess, it falls short of creating what it delivers.

I must confess that I have long been in love with the powers of the mind. Before I was introduced to the teachings of Self-realization, I regarded the intellect and its reasoning capability as paramount among the gifts I was given. To my way of thinking, thinking outranked all other means of learning. I thought, therefore I was! But what I was, was plainly unaware of the extent to which I was deluded.

If ever someone thought that he could think his way to enlightenment, I was the someone. I was well read and well rounded, intellectually curious, analytical, logical—all the qualities that a formal academic education is designed to instill in the student. I could argue a point from various perspectives, and was therefore convinced that I was on the right track. The trouble is, I was unschooled in the art of intuitive wisdom and attunement to a higher consciousness than my own.

The battle for me continues. My head wrestles with my heart and soul for control, and it still prevails much of the time, perhaps because it prefers the structural tidiness that analytical thinking tends to produce. There are questions, however, that give me pause. When I think of Jesus, for instance, chastising the Pharisees for their blind adherence to the niggling rules and demands of Jewish law, would my desire for structure have made me a Pharisee too? And what are the petty rules today that I have not disavowed? Where is my thinking at odds with the possibility of greater understanding, forgiveness, compassion, or generosity? In what ways am I still a Pharisee, clinging to certain coveted social positions to the detriment of my higher potential?

James Barrie, who gave us Peter Pan, once said that "Life is a long lesson in humility." What makes it that is sometimes a matter of our ignorance, but more often, I suspect, it's because we're afraid to let go of thinking that other people and things are supposed to be as we prefer. We develop "rules of engagement." Thus, like Pharisees, we manage to take a teaching on love, for example, little by little adding conditions to it until love is defined mainly by its dependent clauses. Maybe the people we love, in order to stay in our favor, need to think as we do. Maybe they need to act and even dress in accordance with our personal standards.

This practice is called judgment, and we exercise it relentlessly, especially at the subtle levels of our subconscious conditioning. Our teachings tell us that everything is God, and that joy is in finding communion with all things, but by golly, I've got a few ideas of my own that God must have overlooked when He gave *you* the freedom to act as you please!

Yes, indeed, life is a long lesson in humility when that sort of thinking instructs our point of view, because we control but a tiny portion of what goes on around us. Yet, we do not have to be at the mercy of our subconscious programming. We can change with just a firm commitment not to be reactive when the unexpected occurs, or when someone pushes one of our emotional buttons.

It has been wisely said that 10% of life is what happens to us, and that 90% is how we act in response. Do you want to be happy? Take a tip from Sister Gyanamata, who was Paramhansa Yogananda's most advanced woman disciple. Her daily prayer was a single, humble request: "Lord, change no circumstance of my life, change me." When you pray for things to be different instead of the wisdom to accept them as they are, you are just reinforcing your own unhappy reaction to a situation that has come to you for a purpose, a situation that you no doubt invited and need to resolve.

All the great ones who have come again to earth to help us advance, have said it is our destiny to find our freedom in God. Indeed, it is our birthright. We are made of God's consciousness, and since God is fully enlightened, that capacity was born right into us. So, how in the world did things get so messed up? How have we been led so far astray of the glory that is ours to claim?

The monkey wrench in this whole earthly arrangement is that little voice in our heads known as the ego. Descartes had one too. You will find the ego addressed in other essays in this book, but for now let's acknowledge that it can also be a vital friend, helping us to grow in confidence and courage, steering us to all kinds of successes. But when it gets too full of itself, like a Pharisee, it tries to pull us away from aiming for higher awareness and from answering our soul's call. And as a result, we suffer. Whether one is a genius or mentally slow, it comes down to incomplete thinking. We simply cannot understand or undo our inadequacies with the same mind that causes them in the first place.

When Jesus was accused of heresy for asserting his oneness with God, he answered, "Does not your Scripture say that ye are gods?" That divine potential is part of our very nature. God has become us. We are His children, and all we have to do is remember to think and act with that in mind.

BLINDED BY THE MIND

Although we are immortals who are lodged in mortal bodies, most of us dread that death is bound to strip us of our temporal attire, leaving us lifeless at eternity's door. It is in that mortal state of mind, identified with fear and sorrow, that we ordain our return to this physical plane, cast into another frame and cover of mortal garb, for yet another go-round of karmic spin.

Never was there a time when we were not. Nor can there be a time when we will cease to be. And still we bury this news like Jurassic remains, under layers of attachment to earthly dreams, misunderstanding the purpose and wonder of life.

In the Bhagavad Gita, Arjuna surveys the citizen army of his senses that obstruct his path to Self-realization. At first, in despair, refusing to fight, he lays down his bow and his arrows. "They are my kin," he declares to Lord Krishna, "I cannot kill them." In that moment, he, as we, abandons his resolve to free his soul from its physical, mental, and emotional confinement.

Brave are they who do not balk at striving to overcome the lure of our senses. Our senses are family. They are the source of what we know of the world, the bringers and begetters of our worldly ambitions, talents, and wins. But they also lead us into limitation. Seldom do we notice how they become the source of our binding habits, the cause of our pain and confusion, and the denier of truths unseen. We believe what they tell us.

Blessed are they who see in the heart of existence that all is One.

Unity is not a sensory experience. Who can say in looking at a chair and the person sitting on it that oneness is what he perceives? The senses assign to each a name, and to names are added descriptions. Soon no thought is given to both as expressions of the same divine composition. I, in writing these words, have engaged in the same delusion, recording my thoughts as if each belonged to itself and most of all to me. I can even produce the sensory "facts" to prove it!

Blessed are they who muster the courage to act on the soul's behalf.

In this age of secular, fundamentalist noise, the person who answers the call of his soul, ditching social demands and religious dogma, is clearly subversive. He is offered no conventional support in his quest. He may even become the target of convention's alarm and reprisal.

At the end of the first chapter of the Bhagavad Gita, when Arjuna declines to wage battle against his egoic, sensory conditioning, Krishna's reply is the substance of the entire seventeen chapters that remain. It deals with the meaning of life, the nature of action, and the higher-than-earthly aims that each of us must fight to achieve. Arjuna, once changed, begins the war to vanquish the citizens of his mind who were born of ego-consciousness: material desire, selfishness, greed, anger, pride, fear of death, habit born of attachment, and more. Indeed, it is the mind fed of the senses that is the battlefield itself.

The essential teachings of the Gita can be found in the Old Testament, in the Sermon on the Mount, and in all true scriptures. The story is told in symbols in all of these sacred texts as a guide to the Promised Land of reunion with God. The trouble is, until we grasp and act upon its hidden levels of meaning, it is just another fascinating story. And as the world turns, it continues to turn us away from what will free us.

Blessed are they who see with eyes uplifted, unafraid of what only seems.

------♦•◈•♦------

How is one to make sense of this life? It's a moving target that never seems to change, and yet changes all the time: *all* the time and *everywhere*, from cell to shining sea.

Duality is the governor that life on earth obeys. There is no other law that can challenge it for consistency of command. Up and down we go, unaware from day to day that "zero" will be the final result of our merely mortal ventures. Duality ordains it so.

Still, we persist in our sense-making endeavors. We string together the episodes of our lives, reviewing the failures, successes, and juxtapositions, striving by mighty mental computation to understand the various parts and the whole. But life does not yield its secrets to sense-making endeavors. Experience of a higher nature is the key that unlocks the vault wherein this knowledge resides. The mind itself cannot do it.

If you would make sense of this life, study the lives of saints, and then take what you learn into your inner sanctuary of silence, where duality no longer presides, where secrets are revealed.

------♦•◈•♦------

CHAPTER 10

Into the Great Within

"Even a little practice of this inward religion will
free one from dire fears and colossal suffering."

Lord Krishna in the *Bhagavad Gita*

DARE TO BE DIFFERENT
... and a world of difference will emerge

A cts of bravery, important discoveries, and extraordinary events are celebrated by all. But who bravely celebrates with enlightened awareness his own many mistakes? More often we greet them with moodiness, denial, excuse, embarrassment, or even self-defense.

A mistake should be an overture to progress. We grow as we correct what fails to work. Yet, as everyone knows, the reversing of slips and faults can proceed at a snail's pace. Especially at the level of global affairs. Witness, for example, today's frequent eruptions of ethnic and religious strife. "Fails to work" would seem to be the objective!

Ours is an era that cries aloud for a new, inspired expression of unity and understanding. Cultures, countries, and individuals oppose one another on the basis of entrenched beliefs, unwilling to perceive as artifice the dogmas and details that hold them apart. To see these divisions for what they are—vanities and adversities born of ego—is a step in the right direction, but problems that are solved in the mind alone are problems that stay unsolved.

More and more we have turned to science for answers to issues that tend to reveal its intrinsic limitations. Science is committed to facts, empirical data, and material reality. It cannot deliver a transcendent experience, nor does its survival-of-the-fittest theology foster cooperation or even ethical behavior. Science is hardly the genie that will grant us an end to such mistakes as greed, bigotry, war, and reckless abuse of the precious resources that sustain us.

What, then, can make the difference? What can bring us together in ways that capture the heart and stir the soul?

As those of us at Ananda have been blessed to discover, the means to harmony is ever at hand. Meditation as a spiritual practice, far more than a remedy for stress, offers an inner experience that enlightens and changes lives. Further, it kindles a feeling of oneness that heals and dissolves the grievances that divide us. Who, after all, having tasted the sweetness that deep meditation imparts, would prefer the bitter menu of conflict and despair? Surely in meditation there is greater hope for the cause of human accord, and for one's own welfare, than any legislation, political force, or rigid doctrine can provide.

Consider, too, that meditation bridges the gap between peoples of different faiths. As a form of self-offering, it is nonsectarian, ecumenical, and uniquely individual. Indeed, it fulfills the purpose of all religions, for the aim of meditation is divine communion.

While none of us imagines that meditation will suddenly acquire universal acceptance, its power to free us "from dire fears and colossal suffering" is manifestly clear, especially in spiritual communities such as ours. Our good fortune in being drawn to Ananda is a gift of quintessential grace. As Swami Kriyananda would say, without exaggeration, what we are doing at Ananda is the most important work on the planet today.

Here we strive to see the world with more than our physical senses, and with more than our reasoning minds. Meditation reveals the how and why. It also brings into crystal focus for me a quote from James Thurber: "There are two kinds of light: the glow that illuminates and the glare that obscures."

The chances are probably nil that any of us will see an end to the "glaring" social and political mistakes that keep getting recycled. Nor does this age of energy, Dwapara Yuga*, promise major advances in consciousness either. But thankfully with a practice of meditation, we can learn to "stand unshaken" amid the crashing of old, faulty designs and patchwork repairs. And we can make those post-Dwapara advances here and now.

Several years ago my wife Tushti and I spent a week at Ananda Village in Meditation Teacher Training. One of the program's last days was devoted to ways of bringing meditation into daily life. For me these captured meditation's ultimate objective: to live its inner experience from minute to minute, regardless of where or under what conditions. One of those ways is a willingness to acknowledge and appreciate our mistakes, honestly and free of judgment, as a means to moving beyond them more quickly, correctively, gratefully, and joyfully.

---

* Yugas are repeating cycles of time, based on a cosmic span of 24,000 years. Kali Yuga is the age of matter, Dwapara Yuga the age of energy, Treta Yuga the age of consciousness, and Satya Yuga the age of spiritual enlightenment. According to Sri Yukteswar, we are currently in the early ascending phase of Dwapara Yuga, a period of 2400 years. Reference: *The Yugas* by Joseph Selbie and David Steinmetz.

The craziness that characterizes much of today's news stems from people's adherence to old, incompetent logic when it comes to addressing recurrent ills and disputes. Never has this logic succeeded in creating what everyone wants: peace, prosperity, and a life unfettered by dogmas and decrees. Short of requiring all government leaders to learn and practice meditation too, nothing of real consequence is apt to alter the "fails to work" systems that remain in place. The obvious will continue to lie unnoticed, or at least un-acted upon, by those in command. But we *can* make a huge difference inwardly and around us by meditatively practicing Sister Gyanamata's daily prayer: "Change no circumstance in my life. Change me." It works.

Welcome To The Monkey House

Early in his literary career, famous American author Kurt Vonnegut wrote a number of short stories that were later published in a book entitled *Welcome to the Monkey House*. One of those stories is about a character named Harrison Bergeron. It's a futuristic tale, set in a time of excessive government control of people's rights, somewhat like the Big Brother society that George Orwell created in his novel *1984*.

Harrison Bergeron had the misfortune of being above average in intelligence. This meant that he had to be "equalized," lest he become a threat to the status quo. Thus, he was arrested on orders of the U.S. Handicapper General, and disadvantaged in a most ingenious way. His normal brain function was electronically interrupted every six seconds, causing him to forget whatever he had been thinking about, thereby ensuring that he could never think about anything long enough to effectively plot against the people in power.

Well, my own brain, as far as I know, has been spared such a forced alteration, but nevertheless I can relate to young Harrison's predicament. You see, when I sit to meditate, it often seems about every six seconds that a new mental interference tries to scramble my concentration, and cause me to lose my meditative focus! Maybe your focus stays with you longer, but I'm guessing that I am not the Lone Re-arranger of brainwave activity!

Perhaps you can also relate to this. Although most of these distractions of mine come in the form of rather predictable content—such as mentally running through my latest to-do list or trying to remember where I left my keys—sometimes these invasive thoughts have no bearing whatsoever on anything relevant to my present life. They seem to just come out of nowhere, as if they belonged to somebody else. Isn't it true that we all have a certain "weirdness quotient" that cannot be explained in any other terms? A bizarre image or thought comes waltzing in, and we are left to wonder how in the world we could have conjured it up.

And then, almost in the same breath, I find myself reminded of what Yogananda said about our thoughts: that each of them is universally rooted. In other words, no matter how random, remote, or insanely comical my thoughts may appear to be, I have managed to attract them according to my specific level of consciousness. Now that's a little scary!

Speaking for all of us, let me state the obvious: Welcome to the monkey house! Given our social conditioning, no one is completely immune to subconscious interruptions of both a common and outlandish nature. We take in so much data— some of it willingly and a lot of it not—that we're bound to experience a mental intermingling of the information, such that sometimes a vision or thought that unexpectedly pops into our heads can appear as if it came from an alien culture. Viewed from a healthy perspective, at least this can be amusing.

The point I want to make relates to meditation, and despite my obtuse way of getting to it, I hope you find some encouragement in it.

In meditation, you're supposed to relax even as you sit erect. In other words, it's already a test of your discipline, which can make it a test of your attitude and mood. At times you will have meditations that seem like an unrelenting series of detours on a busy road. Does this mean your practice is failing? that you should just hang it up and dive headlong into something that is ego-driven instead? Absolutely not.

Nothing of value was ever won without a firm commitment of energy and willingness. When you make that commitment and hold to it, success accumulates one step at a time. It may not be dramatic, but it will be steady, and it will serve you better than you can imagine at first.

Meditation starts with showing up. It proceeds from a resolution to give it an honest effort. And even in the throes of restless distraction, it earns good karma points for staying the course. When those restless episodes intrude, be mindful of what St. Teresa of Avila said about such occasions: A meditation is well done even if all you did was struggle against those fidgety thoughts that tried to pull you away. Be mindful, too, of what we repeat every Sunday in our Festival of Light: "Even a little practice of this inward religion (meditation) will free one from dire fears and colossal suffering."

Take heart. Let these inspiring words be your incentive, especially when your body and mind are opposed to the whole idea. My wife and I used to practice the martial art of karate. We were blessed to have as our primary instructor a *shihan* who was both a Japanese champion and, more importantly, a man who approached his teaching from a deeply spiritual motivation. He would often begin his class with a question, essentially the same one that Master would loudly ask whenever he took the stage before a lecture: "How feels everyone?" And then he would reply to the question himself: "You feel good or you feel bad, makes no difference. When enemy come, if you no fight, maybe you die."

What he was telling us, of course, is that karate is a metaphor for life, no more and no less than every other discipline under the sun. From music to quantum mechanics to meditation, the demands of the practice are essentially the same. We live each moment fully, with energy and right attitude, or it becomes an opportunity lost. Figuratively speaking, we "die" to the chance we were given to make spiritual progress.

Whether or not we manage to prevail in a worldly sense of the word, we win at what we are doing every moment of doing our best. Did you hear the sound of AUM or see the spiritual eye? Some people do, some don't. Is one group better than the other? This is simply the wrong question to consider. Success in meditation is measured not by phenomena, but rather by how it changes you in all facets of your life. Meditation is certain to prove a battle from time to time, but when you sit for it faithfully, it is bound to have a positive effect on who you are becoming.

So, don't get hung up on the good, the bad, and the ugly of your daily practice. When it comes to meditation, the do-or-die is mostly about your willingness to make the effort, and the attitude you bring to the time you spend. When your willingness and attitude are right, they create a magnetic field of attraction for God's and Guru's grace to carry you forward in subtle yet significant ways.

The monkey house is real. Our minds are in it much of the time. But we don't have to identify with its restless highs and lows, its chatter, or its herd mentality. We can be *in* it, not *of* it.

The Handicapper General is real too. His name is Western society, that sly force that is constantly besieging us with what it says we need to be happy and successful. It does not have your interest at heart, only its own. When you understand that, and when you begin to realize that freedom lies in walking the path that saints and great masters have revealed to us—calmly accepting the challenges that are yours to meet, finding the courage to love and forgive—no handicap can keep you from your destiny: the promise of merging back into union with God.

Every saint and master has been where we are now. They know all about the monkey house, because they grappled the same as we against the same adversities. From the deepest love, needing only our attunement to them, they are ready to guide us across the sea of delusion, around the storms and snags of everyday stresses and errors, into the land of milk and honey: the experience of eternal Bliss.

Start where you are, give yourself to the journey, and, as Lahiri Mahashaya used to say, *"Banat, banat, ban jai."* Doing, doing, someday done.

WORKING THROUGH THE WOBBLIES

Mark Twain once declared that he loved work so much, he could sit and watch it all day. His remark always draws a chuckle from me as I picture him in a rocking chair on the porch of a stately hotel, savoring his favorite cigar, lazily appraising the bee-like business around him. I suspect, however, the remark did not really describe him except as a wit.

Nor does it speak of me. I love work, and I cannot imagine the day that I would not. But here is the obvious disclaimer: I love the work that I love! Give me a task that appeals to me, and my energy for it will flow for as long as needed. But give me a task at the other end of the spectrum, and whether or not it falls within my range of effort and skill, I confess that I will grumble at first, if only to myself. The end may have its reward, but the journey to it will test my sense of enjoyment and good nature.

What brings this to mind is a helpful article by Gyandev McCord, written in 2005 for *Clarity* magazine. He offers how to revitalize one's meditations when the well has begun to run dry. With self-honesty and humor, Gyandev highlights the subtle mental traps that seem to ensnare us all at one time or another. The question is, what do we do about them? How do we manage to pull ourselves out of the pull to give into apathy? How do we get back on track with a greater sense of purpose and devotion?

The answer, for the most part, is to strive with a brighter attitude and a willingness to turn on the juice. But that's the point where the petulant baby in me wants to throw a fit: "You're doing enough already! This approach is too demanding. It'll take too much time, and maybe it won't pay off. C'mon, let's blow it off." And sometimes I have.

These little reactive tantrums, like sudden squalls, are not uncommon when threats to my comfort zone are proposed. I am not averse to taking risks when the odds are decidedly in my favor; when my confidence, that is, is sufficiently present. But in the absence of that, saying "Yes, I'll do it" is a real stretch. My ego hates to be at the wheel if there's the chance of a crash. I grew to believe, like many, that fear of humiliation was the one to fear the most.

This may seem exaggerated when we're talking of something so private as meditation. I can't say that it isn't. But... "What if I do what he says and nothing changes? What if my heart isn't in it? What if God doesn't respond? It'll make me tense, and then I will probably brood. What if I don't win?"

Well, enough of that. It's got nowhere useful to go, and useless isn't an option. I look at Swami Kriyananda's life, and I can't believe that what I have just considered could have come from someone who aspires to follow his lead. I look at the great souls around me, and I know what they had to do to reach where they are. They worked hard, took chances and pushed ahead when the noisy voice of inertia told them not to. Where would I be without them and the spiritual modeling they do for me?

Sometimes the greatest risk is not to take one, even when the outcome looks a bit murky. Although we may not always be ready to do what must be done when the doing is at hand, hoping we can do without it is folly indeed.

We Americans hate to wait. We are a restless people, busy with many matters and the details they produce. Patience has been devalued by us as a virtue. On line, in traffic, and especially when delays pose a threat to our plans, we tend to fidget and stew, focused mainly on hastening what we have no power to revise.

What is your disposition when you must wait for what you want, when you did not figure you would have to? Mine is still lousy at times, and I, who teach meditation and know about karma, should have a better handle on this by now. We learn early in the West to imagine that time is wasted when not assigned to activity, causing us anxious thoughts as waiting prolongs.

Those of the East must find us amusing in our constant quest to fill the gaps that each day's waiting creates. The careful observer can readily see that we are barely present during much of our zooming from one thing to the next, often deriving more satisfaction from crossing finished items off the list than in the journey to complete them. We are programmed, it seems, not only to act in a hurry, but also to measure our progress by the number of sorties concluded.

As we in the West turn slowly in a more inwardly conscious direction, it is odd that we fail to think of waiting as a meditative opportunity. To relax into the purity of it, abandoning all resistance, is an obvious way to withdraw from sensory distraction and restless mind. Meditation is, after all, the disposition we strive to carry into our everyday lives. Why do we incline to view it as just another of our "to-do list" activities, a technique from which to move on?

CHAPTER 11

Social Rants and Remedies

"The tree that moves some to tears of joy is, in the eyes others,

only a green thing that stands in the way."

William Blake

TREEBONE PARKS

Along the road from Hoquiam north,
They lie in shameful array,
Those fields of scattered body parts,
The left-behind of stumps and trunks and amputated arms.
Like sentries massacred at their posts,
The trees that once presided here
Were severed from their roots and stolen away,
Ransomed to brokers and millers
For the gold in their teeth.

Funereal fog and weeping skies
Cast their veil across each desolate scene
As moss, the mourner, in pity taken,
Dresses the naked debris.
There it is, unburied, unblessed,
The aesthetic of maximum profit at minimum cost.
No peace resides in the stillness here,
Nor Forest Lawn effect to excuse the effect.
In litter of haste, in parks of bones,
No children come to play.

O, lords of logs forgotten, of lumber to burn,
Spare us your speeches of growing more than is gone.

WE ARE ONE WHO SEE TWO

In a 2015 article in the *Times of India*, a gentleman by name of M. Raman wrote that "a true patriot transcends geography." He sought further to make the case that patriotism and religious allegiance are kindred, and that in the best of worlds, each would serve the greater good of all.

This might be true, but we do not live in the best of worlds, and two of the main reasons are patriotism and religious allegiance. Both are expressions of worship, one being a national or tribal loyalty, the other a loyalty-link to God. While these two fidelities deserve a certain praise, when carried too far—as we see almost everywhere today—they breed an attitude of exclusivity, pitting countries and creeds against those of other loyalties and beliefs.

Patriotism and religious conviction are clearly at the root of hatred and strife in most global areas of unrest, proving how susceptible they can be to extreme beliefs and fanatical behaviors. They are two sides of the same undisciplined zeal that leads to misunderstanding, suspicion, dissonance, and an ultimate poverty of spirit. If the world is ever to be a single family, devoted to the welfare of all beings, the jingoistic ways of patriotism and religion will have to lose their appeal and, like the dinosaur, become extinct.

Such will almost certainly not happen soon. Though pride comes before the fall, it is still ascendant today in the form of patriotic and religious extremism. Civil and multi-national wars, reflected in the fervor of sports rivalries also, are fomented as if they were righteous no matter the cost. Enemies are created where none exist except to give a sense of superiority and false honor to those taking sides. It's a loser's game for the winners too.

Love of country, and love of how we are taught to connect with God, are etched into us from an early age. We accept our homeland and heavenly path as blessings of our birth, as members of a special clan, and we pledge ourselves to the symbols of their values: flag, faith, scriptural text, rituals, and traditions. But this ferments into feelings of us and them, and "them" becomes the cause of what we dislike that is not of us.

Unity has long been a buzzword in pleas for peace and accord by well-meaning statesmen around the world, and by well-meaning religious leaders as well, but as long as it is sought in efforts to eliminate people's basic differences, unity will fail. To succeed it must respect and absorb our cultural, ethnic and sexual dissimilarities.

When Paramhansa Yogananda went to the West in 1920, and for 32 years thereafter as he vigorously promoted the ways and means to Self-realization, he also envisioned the dawning of a United States of the World. His concept of this was not foreseen as homogenized or utopian, but rather as a diverse cultural mix of people devoted to the ideals of community: cooperative instead of competitive, spiritual instead of religious or materialistic, dedicated to the truth of "Yato dharma, tata jaya"—Where there is right action, there is victory.

Small, self-sustaining colonies were the model in Yogananda's mind for these united "states," where residents would incorporate home, work and worship in one place. Founded by Swami Kriyananda years later, eight of these successful communities offer long-standing proof that we can and must live together in an atmosphere of mutual support, emphasizing that people are more important than things. No other so-called solution can hope to undo the madness of today's congested cities and the tension-filled, wretched existence that most of their inhabitants are forced to accept as normal. The alternative is more of the same, made worse by mini and macro wars over ever-diminishing resources, fueled in large part by patriotic and religious fanatics.

A patriotic attitude toward humanity as a whole, and religious guidance steeped in compassion for all, must begin to take the lead in place of the "I, me, mine" mentality that prevails today. Nations and religions serve their purpose only in standing for tolerance and rhetorical restraint. Allegiance born of dogma and indoctrination is a danger waiting to strike. Spirituality alone—free of sectarian bias, free of institutional control, free of caste, creed, or class—can turn love of country and love of God into a marriage that will endure for the benefit and bliss of all.

ALMOST A POEM, EVER A PLEA

Wake up and smell the harsh winters ahead, my fellow consumers.
The air is putrid with rotten plans to push the envelope
Into the looming abyss. Mother has had enough of our excuses.
Now it is we who are the ones at stake.
The time has come, and is nearly gone, to
Let the earth breathe free of our reasoning's mischief,
Free of our poking, probing, pumping, dumping, cutting, paving,
And polluting for trophies of greed.
Let us look to our needs, our modesties, and no more.
And let us not confuse them with everything else:
Kardashians, golden parachutes, and government pork,
Imitation public schools and toxic student bodies,
Imitation foods and toxic corporate minds.
Let the marketers raise the flag of constructive living at last,
Harmonious with the silent, diminishing resources that sustain us.
Let science and business and political schemes be focused on saving and
Nurturing what we have left.
Let them find their profit in that, or let the bleeding begin.
Let hurricanes come, and major quakes, and the spew of reborn volcanoes,
And drought and famine, melting polar ice and rising tides, and cruel winds.
We have earned them all, and they will carry the day.
Katrina was just a messenger, calling for a truce.
Others will follow more quickly now until the truce is made.
One way or another, harmony will be restored.
But who of us will be around to realize the lesson? \
Pray it will be the repentant.

A SHORT HISTORY OF THE U.S. IN VIETNAM

On the tenth anniversary of troop withdrawal, April 30, 1985

Counselors came and the counsel was bad,

And the Government called it good.

The good came and gave what they had,

And the Government called for more.

More came and razed the land,

And the Government called it required.

More and more came and more and more fell,

And the Government called for more.

Critics came and doubt was cast,

And the Government called them to blame.

The enemy came and came and came,

And the Government called it quits.

The end came that would not end,

And the Government called it a win,

And called it peace.

Dealing with Trouble

Are we ever safe from trouble? Apparently not. If my karma doesn't trigger it, someone else's will (which, I suppose, makes it my karma too).

The trouble is, trouble has fuel to spare, and it can even run on fumes. Trouble is also deceptive. Innocent disguise and seductive appeal are two of its most ingenious masquerades. Every day, aided by anyone seeking to shortcut the road to personal gain, trouble hits the headlines and shapes the news. And so it is never in short supply of allies or unwary victims.

But doesn't it seem that trouble today is more plentiful and potent than just a few decades ago? Beyond the occasional karmic bomb and mean-spirited assault, there seems to be a general escalation in short-term stupidity and its long-term effects. Gaps of time without trouble are quickly filled with newly created socio-economic, environmental, pharmaceutical, chemical, or biological disasters, each inventively exacerbated by political intervention. Even where there might be an absence of these, the media manages to feed our fears that such will occur any moment, and so wannabe troubles become troubles in fact.

It seems fair to say that our world has fallen off the edge of balance, and those who have workable plans to correct our tilt are, alas, not the ones we target for remedial help. Protesters march, picket, and rave for legislative changes to solve inequities that legislation is genetically incapable of solving.

Every four years we elect a president to lead us in putting right our errors and wrongs, and he, under pressure from those committed to weary old standards, relies on the same procedures and organizations to address what needs to be done. Bureaucracy runs the country, and the country suffers to feed the beast its every growing due. Does anyone believe that trouble will retire to playing a lesser role so long as we invest our hopes in political answers to problems?

I take heart in the firm belief that someday the social and political models that Americans accept today will finally be supplanted by practical, holistic alternatives that do not require rhetoric to recommend them. As often foretold by a great saint and master, Paramhansa Yogananda, the solution already exists in the ether. Small cooperative communities, he said, will spring up like natural cures from organic seeds of social and moral intelligence, and their value systems will create a new imperative. "People are more important than things" will be the message they carry. And for some, the most successful, the bonding will have its basis in seeking God; not in a structured religious sense, but rather in a supportive way that leads each person inward to realize the fullness of his potential. This is the holistic paradigm, inspired by Yogananda and put into practice by Swami Kriyananda, that has already existed for nearly fifty years on a small but vibrant scale: the self-governing community at the margins of normal society.

Trouble, of course, does not disappear even with the best arrangements of people, precepts, and policies. We are bound to our human imperfections, and to a physical plane where duality prevails as plainly as night and day, and where virtue must bear the weight of its counterbalance. But a blessing to all is he who strives in himself to live outside the materialistic emphasis of today. It is he, living in community with others of his kind, who points the way to a freer future, freer of troubles that do not have to repeat.

FOOD FOR THOUGHT

In the summer of 1990, during the annual Mozart Festival in Salzburg, Austria, my wife and I were staying with a new friend in his apartment. Richard had lived in Salzburg for many years, retired from his long-time career as the personal secretary to Herbert von Karajan, the famous Berlin Philharmonic conductor. Aristocratic society had been his world, but now Richard was serving the homeless a couple of times a week at a soup kitchen run by Franciscans. He, himself, had become a lay brother.

One particular "patron" of the kitchen, a bitter alcoholic, was invariably abusive in his language and manner, always demanding more soup and bread than he was given, thankless of the generosity that Richard and the other volunteers were willing to provide. Richard never replied to the man except with more food and maybe a kind remark. I could not understand this. It upset me to observe or hear about it, and part of my anger was aimed at Richard for not telling him off. The Franciscan way of unconditional love was beyond my mental and emotional grasp. To me it was stupid.

But I did notice this: Richard was happy.

I cannot say that I have learned the lesson of this experience completely. I still react at times when confronted with belligerence, rudeness, or a selfish demand. And, of course, I am the one who suffers the toxic effect. To see a hateful person as a child of God is one heck of a challenge.

But this I have also noticed: Selfish people are never happy, no matter how often their demands are met. And unselfish, service-minded people do not suffer the sting of others' ill-mannered assaults. What a concept!

Attunement to our highest potential, non-attachment to the fruits of desire— Oh, my, these are testy aims, because we are steeped in delusion above all else. Our society drives us to strive ever more for that which is hopelessly mortal, to believe that people and things are the source of joy. We're conditioned to ask of every choice, "What's in it for me?" And so it is that our highs turn into lows, and our lows turn into longings and strivings for new highs that are yet of the same soon-to-perish likeness.

Surely the most amazing part of this whole human journey back to God is the length of cosmic time it takes us to quit our worldly ways. In the lexicon of oxymorons, "intelligent man" ranks among the best. Richard had not forsaken the fleeting pleasures of outward living. He relished many common pursuits, and he fully enjoyed their yield. His Franciscan spirit, however, kept them in perspective, when otherwise his appreciation of them would have fled.

"Think outside the box," we are told when the box confines our creativity, especially in seeking solutions to difficult problems. This is good advice, of course, but other good advice would be to think more intelligently *inside* the box in the first place, in particular when designing the box itself. If that were commonly done, plenty of room would be left within its boundaries for innovation, artistic expression, and efficiency.

A lack of formal education is widely underrated, especially as it tends to prevent disasters that only an educated person could reason his way into.

The unschooled man or woman, limited to rendering simple solutions to life's basic problems, is likely to avoid considering or dealing with complex social issues. Thus, these issues are generally left to people of superior intellect and scholarship to resolve. And as a result, they are frequently raised to greater degrees of complexity, finally attaining an apex of sophisticated absurdity and illogic.

Love, generosity, compassion, and simple wisdom are clearly no match for brainy ideas when it comes to settling disputes, serving the needy, or saving the planet. Only an educated intelligentsia, motivated by the lure of personal gain or the fear of personal loss, could produce the state of affairs that exists today in the Middle East, in the halls of legal justice worldwide, in the compromised atmosphere that encircles us, in the earth and oceans that nourish us, and in the minds of those who live by the dogmas and slogans of privilege and self-importance. It is this, if we are to be undone, that will bring about our undoing.

Many fear what may lie ahead: loss of income, loss of love, physical decline, diminished mental capacity, chronic illness and, of course, the end of life as we know it. It seems that nothing is more effective at reducing the length and quality of one's existence than giving into worries about what could go wrong as we age. To the extent that we buy into it, not only do we suffer from what has yet to occur, we energize with our fears the potentialities we dread.

Once upon an ancient time, when humanity's survival demanded cooperation, the individual ego was blessedly underdeveloped. Competition, political committees, and complicated bureaucratic systems were yet unborn, because impasse and opposition were unaffordable choices. Today, however, we have conquered these limitations, evolving to a level of comfort that can seemingly tolerate astonishing stupidities in the name of national pride and social expedience.

Democracy may be our best hope for the future of our existence, but America's particular brand of it has descended in practice to a shadow of what is presumed by the word's definition. To say that it is superior to the systems of other countries is a recommendation that falls severely short of being effective. The reason is clear. We have set in motion a staggering series of troubles, which our leaders insist can be remedied with more of the same thinking that caused them in the first place: more money, more political muscle, more consumer supply and demand, more advanced technology, and more centralization of control. These are plainly the ingredients of a recipe for calamity and ruin.

"My country, right or wrong" is a jingoistic idea that should have been blasted to smithereens the day it was first saluted. Leadership in America—and everywhere else, for that matter—needs an extreme makeover. The most visible result of our two-party governing process, at the federal rank especially, is that each political side, driven to prove the other unfit to rule, consistently succeeds in making the point.

A rotted hull of a craft is the USS Political State of Affairs, adrift in a storm of its own whip and toss, sinking loudly in a swirling sea of words, pretending badly to know of where it is bound. Captains, o' many captains, confess to the harm of your steerage, and let us be. With staff and crew, abandon ship that we may settle into the calm of your absence, that we may survive to rescue ourselves by necessary remembrance of how to sail as one. We can do no worse without you, and if by chance we fail, at least it will be in waters undisturbed by the sweep of your furious winds of gainless partisan howl.

———————

The world is round. Round and round it goes. Life, however, is linear. It goes from here to there, and then it repeats. Thus, in this peculiar place, that which is alive goes round and round in a linear manner.

For many people this is very confusing. In their linear way of thinking, they cannot wrap their minds around the roundness. It does not come to a point, they say. Therefore neither do they. They live from day to day, until the end of their linear stretch, inventing little pursuits to pass the time: fame, fortune, power, comfort, and most of all, drama.

Clearly, what is needed is a world with a real point, which would motivate people to move in its direction. Love? Wisdom? Peace? God? Oneness? Somehow these have never been roundly accepted as better aims. Apparently it is easier to remain confused and pointlessly self-absorbed.

———————

CHAPTER 12

Almost Everything Else

"All that we are is the result of what we have thought."

The Buddha

Language is often considered our greatest tool, enabling us to share complex ideas, news of our world, and personal thoughts. Other creatures are limited to basic signals of sound and pitch, which confines their communication to the merely instinctual. We are clearly their superiors when it comes to invention, sophistication, and subtlety of expression. Nor can they match our talent for misunderstanding.

Life is shadow and light. You can dwell in either one. Where do you think you are? Where do you want to be? What are you thinking?

From thoughts repeated are habits born, and so the past repeats. History itself becomes a tedious mixture of old mistakes, molded as if into plaster to prevent its variation. Why do we doubt that we can make a difference? Why do we fear to break the mold when life is ever new? What are we thinking?

Learning to Forget

There's a funny one-liner that bemoans the effects of aging: "Of all the things I've lost, I miss my mind the most." Thank goodness for humor. It softens the blow.

Uhh. . . Let's see now. . . Where was I going with that? . . . Oh, yes. . . As some of us know already, seniors are forced to deal with a hitch that gets hitchier as years go by. Suddenly, at the darnedest times, our Random Access Memory begins to flash "Access Denied."

Actually, though, the real problem lies in the other direction. Losing our mind is all too rare an event. Doggedly, it clings to us like a magnet made of chatter. As Eckhart Tolle has written in *The Power of Now*, the inability to stop thinking has become "a dreadful affliction," but since almost everyone suffers from it, we take it as normal.

The truth is, nothing comes between us like our very own mental activity. Restlessly, it denies us the experience of oneness with all that is. From moment to moment, wherever we turn, our senses recognize *this* and *that* as unrelated to *me*. Thus, believing that separation exists, we have managed to turn this Garden of Eden into a kind of Marx Brothers asylum.

Because we've been given the blessed burden of five physical senses, almost all of our data is gathered from their reports. Analysis ensues. Likes and dislikes arise. And so we career like pinballs between bumpers of pleasure and pain. For most of us the game goes on and on until we die.

But the greater trouble is deeper than even our sensory involvement. As we slalom through our days, supposedly using our minds to some intelligent purpose, we fail to see that, like double agents, they have been *using us*, relentlessly feeding us fears and desires that trigger more of the same. Without the means to quiet our barnstorming thoughts—namely through full engagement in the flow of now—we are fated to fidgety, fickle-brain commotion and the onset of moods.

There's a poem by the Indian master Thayumanavar that puts the problem in perspective. Included are these lines: "You can ride a lion; You can play with the cobra; You can make vassals of the gods; You can walk on water and live in fire; But control of the mind is better and more difficult."

The question naturally arises: Why can't we train our minds to tame the distracting fears and aches that besiege us? The answer: because *the mind is the problem!* "Imagine a chief of police trying to find an arsonist," says Tolle, "when the arsonist *is* the chief of police."

We are dealing here with the ego, of course, a most unscrupulous opponent. As we become identified with our emotions and thoughts, the force of ego presides over all that we do. It uses the past to define us and the future to distract us.

The trick is to stay in the present, a trick that few can perform. It requires that we refuse to judge whatever the present brings. But as we are able to do this—to observe the moment without shading its character—a transformation takes place that makes it instantly friendlier.

Yogananda said, "Circumstances are always neutral." The universe assigns no value to what unfolds. Energy has no opinion. It is merely our reaction to each condition that gives it a plus or minus on the tally sheet we carry around in our heads, confining us to the grasp of our wishes and worries. What a waste!

Living in the present is a kind of constructive forgetting. By saying "Yes" to the moment, time and its accretions dissolve, especially those of self-concern. And surprisingly when this occurs, success in matters of worldly endeavor is achieved more easily also.

Forgetting is inevitable, and frankly, it is often a blessing. My father, until he was well into his eighties, had a memory that selected mainly the things that upset him, whether about himself or other people. But as his memory faded, submitting at last to Alzheimer's disease, he found less and less to disturb his increasing quietude. I like to think that when he died, he had made a peace with himself that only forgetting could accomplish. Or perhaps, hoping for the best, I should say that what he finally remembered was the sweetness and serenity of his ego-obscured soul.

Great masters admonish us to lose our minds in God. Strive to unlearn, they counsel, the mortal ideas that lead us to material attachments and selfish pursuits.

By scientific as well as spiritual law, these are bound to bring suffering to balance whatever happiness might be fleetingly achieved.

Jesus said, "Seek ye first the kingdom of God, and all these things shall be added unto you." No, not fancy cars and trophy homes. By "all these things" he meant peace, calmness, wisdom, love, joy and divine communion. We must only practice forgetting to dwell in the past and future, in the consciousness of separation, in worldly desires that offer no lasting value.

Hey, Just Get Over It!

We know what it means to hurt, but are we bound to suffer?

Pain must come. In sudden and chronic experience, in large and small doses, pain is bound to come. Ours is the pain planet. We were born here to feel and deal with pain's discomfort, to endure its seemingly infinite permutations, to confront its huge force.

Until we attain liberation, each turn of the karmic wheel can be counted on to include painful episodes by the hundreds or more. And for humans of highest consciousness, namely those of saintly ways, the tests of mettle only seem to increase. No doubt by celestial design, our most extreme trials are often saved for last. Consider, for example, the long list of Catholic saints who were persecuted severely by the Church itself. Those of deepest faith, like Padre Pio, are often the ones who seem to pose a threat to conventional ways, and are the most abused.

As the lives of these spiritual heroes reveal to us, however, suffering is not a required sequel to pain, persecution, or even terrible loss. Suffering is ever a choice. When we endure it, it's because we allow it: for days, for years, for lifetimes. Can you imagine a more ridiculous and wasteful practice?

The familiar adage, "No pain, no gain," can be applied throughout nature. Birth, survival, and death are painfully demanding. But notice the absence of any reference to suffering. Pain from which a gain is won, like the grain of irritation that produces a pearl, is hardly a cause for misery. Anguish is added merely of unconscious habit.

When a loved one dies, especially if unexpectedly, the pain can seem intolerable at first. Slowly it subsides into mourning, and for some it may often return in visitations of missing what used to be or might have been. But even here, suffering need not steep like leaves of tea in memory's cup. Only in the taint of self-pity does it find a fertile soil for its bitter seed.

Why, then, do we permit ourselves to agonize over so much of what goes on? The short answer is that we are not yet saints. Like hostages to fate, we confine ourselves to a limited potential. The idea that misery could be avoided, even when tragedy strikes, does not easily fit within the scope of our conditioning. Emotion intervenes, leaving us rather to grieve, brood, and blame, meanwhile learning little if at all. It is only when we have had enough of letting our emotions control us that we start to explore beyond the fractured mentality we have accepted.

To suffer is to misunderstand the mission before us. God's love and God's joy are the qualities we are here to express and become. As we sink into suffering's dark embrace, a single question should come to mind, even if we are unprepared to answer it honestly at the time: Is this not a vanity disguised as a wound?

Suffering is, after all, an egotistical, subjective response to a cosmically neutral event. The soul does not demand, invite, or desire it. We, alone, provide the charge to every moment's occurrence that undercuts its otherwise impartial nature. Out of anger, fear, envy, or some other caustic reaction, it is we who ordain that suffering must ensue.

I have heard it said that free will is choosing what we have to do anyway. Suffering, then, is choosing to *resist* what we have to do anyway. Given the failure and frustration that such resistance begets—the colossal evidence of which has accumulated over millennia—one would think we would be deterred from pursuing its fruitless course.

In writing this, I know it is unlikely to have a lasting effect on me or anyone else. The hardest lessons on a spiritual path need many reiterations before they take root in consciousness and behavior. I, myself, continue to struggle with this one.

But here's a story that never fails to remind me of how I could be too.

In the early days of Ananda, a fire destroyed the temple at what is now the Meditation Retreat. Much time and effort had been spent on its construction, and to lose it so soon and so swiftly was a real blow. But only a day or two later, Swami Kriyananda was singing merrily as he strolled the aisles of a local retail store, shopping for basic supplies. The store's owner asked in amazement, "How are you able to sing after such a personal disaster?" Swamiji replied without hesitation, "Madame, I lost a temple, not my voice."

Thank God for the few like him, who reveal to us the courage, wisdom, and grace that abides in giving pain its due and no more. Giving it a place to nest is the only mistake.

Noble Is As Noble Does

In the years I managed our Ananda Pune ashram, the workday began after meditation and breakfast with a morning circle. Tushti and I, with our staff and guests, would discuss the day's projects and assignments, and then we would all affirm together, loudly at first and then more inwardly, "I will do my work thinking of Thee, Lord. I offer to Thee the very best that is in me."

It's too bad that governments and corporations don't do something similar. If they did, and if they took it to heart, we wouldn't need millions of laws and thousands of agencies to enforce them. The Golden Rule would preside, because in offering to God the best that is in us, it becomes our nature to serve our neighbors in that same spirit.

As we strive to do better, the real work is not about building or fixing things, it's about building and fixing ourselves. Attitudes, relationships, and commitments are the greater construction projects involved in creating a successful community, which creates a more successful you and me. A house is not a home if it is just a structure, even if it is a palace. You have to fill it with love and joy, otherwise it is merely a place of temporary shelter. Likewise, a body is not a home if the person living inside is unhappy, lazy, angry, greedy, or selfish. When that is the case, there is work to be done, and who of us can be called a finished product?

We sometimes refer to ourselves as "works in progress." What we need to keep in mind is that a work in progress implies that someone is investing actual work in making the changes necessary for progress to occur!

Building a spiritual community, as we were endeavoring to do, is a gradual, ongoing process too. It takes time. But in fact the idea of community does not require an actual community to exist. You can have it in spirit wherever you are. Community is serving and supporting each other for the welfare of all. It is doing the work of clearing away our egoic motivations. It is offering the best that is in us.

Work done in the right spirit, from the messiest chore to steering the course of a nation, is to me a supremely noble occupation. It nourishes the soul whether or not the outcome is what was hoped for. Work is about the journey more than the destination. Performed with right attitude, it becomes a blessing to the individual and the universe alike.

Oh, but don't we love to complain when work becomes a drag. Have you ever tried to get out of doing work of that sort? Or maybe you cut a corner or two in order to be done with it sooner. Sometimes work gets in the way of how we would rather be spending our time, and we don't exactly give it the "best that is in us."

Years ago, Edgar Bergen was a popular on-stage ventriloquist, whose "dummy" was a little wise-cracker called Charlie McCarthy. Charlie was like the voice of the ego that chatters inside our heads. As part of their comedy routine, Bergen was always making appeals to Charlie's better nature, usually to no avail. Once, in urging Charlie to do a particular job, he said, "Charlie, a little work never killed anyone." Charlie replied, "Yeah, but why take a chance!"

Today it is common for people to work long hours, often under stressful conditions and constant deadlines. For those with families to support, there appears to be no alternative. Instead of finding pleasure in work, the result is more often a growing list of worries and feeling trapped. Even for those who are wealthy, work is mostly a means to an end with little joy in the means, and the end is a fleeting experience that turns to disappointment. We think we are seeking freedom, but the truth is, we are giving it away.

These days, too, many workers are driven by dreams of retiring. Work becomes an endurance test with the goal of having no work at all. But retirement for the purpose of doing very little soon develops into an empty life. Without a diet of constructive goals and activities, the pursuit of fun itself turns futile and unfulfilling.

My father was an excellent physician who loved his medical practice. But when he retired from it at age 70, he did not apply his will to pursuits that would have renewed his spirit. Playing golf and doing crossword puzzles were about the only activities he engaged in, and his world shrank to the space of his limited routines. He failed to see the value of reaching out to others, as he had as a doctor, in some other useful way. And so he just mostly waited with increasing misery for the end to come.

In bold letters on the T-shirt of a senior citizen, the message was loud and clear. "I'm retired," it announced. In smaller print below, it said, "I was tired yesterday, and I'm tired again today." Tired and bored is what happens when we lose our will to contribute to the betterment of our world.

If I ask myself why I was born, the answer in one form or another is essentially the same. It is to "offer to Thee the very best that is in me." This life is a playing field on which I am opposed by my lesser nature. Working to overcome its negativities is not only the way to reach my highest potential, it is also the way to a happier me. Good work drives out our pettiness, our moodiness, our worries.

This is not an easy time to be alive, but we cannot wish away the trials it brings. The great American president Thomas Jefferson was once asked if he believed in luck. He replied that yes, he did. When the interviewer asked him why, Jefferson said that he simply studied the law that luck obeys. "The more good work I do," he said, "the more good luck I have."

What do we know about this life on earth? We know it has been designed as a test: a test of will, a test of courage, a test of attitude and behavior. Every day arrives with a new set of challenges, but virtually all of these are not new at all. They are simply repackaged versions of ones we failed to handle in the past. They are lessons unlearned that continue to cycle back until we do the work of putting them behind us. They're the self-defeating habits we haven't changed, the moods we have yet to overcome, the desires and attachments that bind us to our delusions, and thus to a stream of disappointments, worries, doubts, and suffering.

Every unresolved test is a summons to do the work that is needed in order to pass it. It's a call to the best that is in us, because when we give all that we can, there is growth, there is greater freedom, there is inner peace and joy.

Why is a person ever unhappy? There are two possibilities: he is ignorant (unaware) of the cause, or he remains unwilling to change the effect. Courage must be mustered, will power must be applied, and action must be taken. These issues are not complex, but so often we would rather make excuses than do what we have to. Maybe we're confused, and we seek advice. This can be a wise choice unless, as the case may be, it is merely a stalling tactic. The author Erica Jong had this to say about seeking the opinion of others in personal matters. "Advice is what we ask for when we already know the answer and wish that we didn't."

If you do your best, will you get whatever you work for in this world? Not a chance. If that were true, who would aspire for Self-realization? We would be seduced into thinking that lasting happiness is possible on earth, which it is not. God's intent in thwarting our ambitions from time to time is not to deprive us of enjoyment; rather it is to show us where our true enjoyment lies: in seeking Him.

"I will do my work thinking of Thee, Lord. I offer to Thee the very best that is in me." Affirm it, put your willingness and energy into it, and you will discover a freedom, an inner peace, and a joy that exceeds in quality and duration any pleasure that can be found in doing less.

COURAGE OF MANY KINDS

Stories of courage are more than merely impressive. They tell of the best that is in us. Images come to mind of heroic deeds, of men and women risking their lives to rescue others from imminent harm, disaster, or death. We think of firemen running into burning buildings to save a mother and child, soldiers charging into enemy fire, or a stranger braving the rush of traffic to snatch a toddler from oncoming cars just in the nick of time.

But what of those acts of courage that are not so publicly obvious? that take place away from the spotlight? that are simply victories of a deeply personal nature? Are they any less important? any less worthy of praise or recognition? Does God see greater value in saving a person from drowning in a turbulent sea than in the courage of an alcoholic to overcome his addiction? It seems to me that when we dare to push ourselves beyond our fears or perceived limitations, whether to save ourselves or someone else, God looks equally at what has been done. We are that someone else too.

In fact, I would say that courageous deeds in response to a sudden emergency are not as demanding as ones that require sustained courage over a period of weeks or even years: such as the courage to fight back from a paralyzing stroke, from a self-destructive habit such as drug abuse, or even from a life of hardbitten criminal behavior.

Swami Kriyananda identified four kinds of courage: (1) blind courage—the kind that is reactive, that we see in sudden, death-defying rescue situations; (2) passive courage, such as the conscious ability to absorb a great financial loss, and to keep going forward without falling apart; (3) dynamic courage, the kind that we see in people who buck the tide of social convention to create a product, a service, or an ideal that breaks the mold and benefits the rest of us. In this latter category are people as diverse in their endeavors as Abraham Lincoln and Steve Jobs.

The fourth kind of courage is what Swami called divine: the courage to live in selflessness and self-offering, devoted to God and the welfare of humankind without attachment to the gains or losses of this earthly experience. Divine courage surrenders to God as the one and only Doer of all that is done, and it seeks no prize except the love and joy that comes of working for Him alone. We might think of Gandhi or Mother Teresa.

The foremost divinely courageous person in my life was Swami Kriyananda himself. To me the greatest lesson in all that he accomplished—and in all that he endured, from decades of illness and physical pain to decades of false accusations and vicious lawsuits—is the inner peace and bliss he displayed no matter what or how much was crashing around him.

But we, who are not so evolved, tend to put divine courage at the bottom of our to-do list. First comes every attempt to exercise our free will in pursuit of material gains, personal callings, and the fruits of our labors. It is only after countless incarnations that we begin to realize the monotony and futility of such pastimes and preoccupations. Slowly, slowly, we tire of the not-so-merry-go-round that we are driven by our desires to endure. Finally we turn our attention to the wisdom, ways, and will of God, finding in this the divine courage to change.

In the meantime, though, we specialize in excuses for why service and surrender to God is not one of our agenda items. "I'm too tired. . . I need a break. . . I don't want others to think I'm weird. . . I think it's important to experience life more fully. . . I think it's unhealthy to deprive myself of activities and things that don't do anyone any harm. . ." and the list goes on. We are very skilled at convincing ourselves that what we want from the world out there is going to serve us usefully. And if it doesn't, we quickly look for something else that might.

Nayaswami Asha tells the story of counseling a woman who insisted that it was essential to have as many desires as possible, so that every time the pursuit of one turned to disappointment, there would be another in the wings right away! She was completely persuaded that this was the most intelligent life strategy. Only by degrees are we any different, still hoping that we can make our pleasures last until the next one of equal intensity comes along.

The trouble is, no indulgence of an external nature can satisfy our deeper longings for inner peace, unconditional love, and durable joy. Hence the tremendous courage it takes to (1) recognize the inherent mistake of buying into the "good life" that society is trying to sell us, (2) resist the enormous pressure that others are bound to apply to us to conform, and (3) be willing to "Go on alone" when others cry, "Your dream is not our own."

Yes, we often stumble, even as aspiring devotees and yogis. We get drawn into detours that put us off track of our destiny, and this is not entirely our fault. The conditioning we receive from the time we are babes in arms is decidedly sensory and outward. We are raised as much by society as by our parents, and chances are, our parents were largely invested in the same set of social standards that informed their generation. When you hear every day that happiness lies in money, power, social position, relationships, and things. . . well, it sinks into our subconscious mind and takes over the show. Not many people have the insight, courage, and strength to see through the falseness of society's premise and steer their lives in a more inward direction.

Any way you slice it, life in this world is hard to redirect when the world itself is where you tend to engage.

But let's throw a little good news into the mix. As someone who is reading this book, you must already be open to having more than a superficial life. You probably also recognize that you alone are responsible for what your life has become, and that no one but you can make it better. Courage starts with that kind of acceptance: acceptance of the life you've created, and of the risks you will need to take to improve it. If you have come to that understanding, and if you are making the effort to practice its wisdom, you are on the Home stretch.

A fifth kind of courage is easy to overlook because we may not think of it as brave, and that is the courage to ask for help when you need it. Sometimes life deals a blow that is too hard to cope with effectively on our own. It may be a physical, emotional, or mental illness, an experience of severe trauma or abuse, or the profound loss of a loved one. We tend to ascribe bravery to those who suffer in silence, but when suffering is prolonged, or when it interferes dramatically with the rest of one's life, then choosing to remain silent is probably more reckless than courageous.

And still there is another form of courage that is highly important to exercise whenever certain situations arise: the courage to speak up when you see or sense that something is not as it should be, especially with regard to people's behavior, and even more especially when you are the person affected by that behavior. When you don't speak up, everyone loses, and nobody learns.

I will end with a little personal story that to me has been very instructive. When I was a boy, I was always scared to hang upside down on a crossbar by my knees. My friends would do it, laughing and having fun, but I was sure it was dangerous, and that I might fall on my head and break my neck. So I never gave it a try. This was not a serious challenge to my self-esteem, and when I grew past the age of playground activities, I forgot about the matter. . . until one night, at the age of 35, as I was walking through a park that had a play area for kids, including a crossbar like the ones of my childhood. No one else was around, and I suddenly decided to dare myself to hang by my knees. As I let go of the bar with my hands and lowered my body into the upside down position, I breathed a happy sigh of relief and smiled with great satisfaction. I was okay. I had done it, and it was indeed kind of fun! I didn't fall on my head, and now I don't have to reincarnate to conquer that childhood fear!

All that is to say, it's never too late to deal with whatever frightens you. Start with the little things, like hanging upside down by your knees, and as your confidence grows, tackle the bigger ones next. What is little or big for each of us is bound to be different by degrees, maybe even very different. But each of us knows what those issues are that are keeping us from the inner peace and contentment we want. Pray for the courage you need. Visualize yourself meeting the test, succeeding, and feeling the joy that comes whenever a heavy burden is lifted. God does not want you to fall on your head, and He will be there for you, holding you up, as you wisely and courageously push through your personal fears and limitations that keep you from moving ever more progressively toward His all-loving embrace.

REMEMBER TO SELF-FORGET

I am of a "certain age," as they say, when memory becomes less reliable. This can be hard to gracefully accept and adjust to. I can recollect as a teen having almost photo recall, when I could bring all kinds of information from storage to speech in an instant. Not so today. I depend to a greater extent on writing notes and lists, which works fairly well when I happen to remember where I've put them!

I try to make light of my lapses—failing to think of a person's name or where I left my keys—but the inconvenience at times can turn to frustration. If you're young and not dealing with this condition yet, trust me, you'll get your chance!

Driving around these days, we are likely to see a now familiar sign: "Road work ahead. Expect delays." This is precisely the message I receive when slowing down to fix a cranial connection that has come apart. Suddenly there's a flagger in the path of my effortless mental acuity with a sign that says, "Stop," and there I am, waiting for the signal to proceed, while the workers in my brain try to repair the link to wherever my thought was going.

Most of us view the decline of memory with a measure of distress. Although it appears to be largely a natural phenomenon, we tend to regret it, often with a sense of vexation and despair. Granted, it can be problematic and sometimes even embarrassing to be forgetful, but in the divine scheme of things, what does it really matter? Is it important for our spiritual welfare to remember the facts, details, and events of this worldly existence? Truly, it is not.

I recently returned from a month-long stay in India. I was traveling alone, this time with more than I could comfortably manage: two 50-lb. suitcases, a 20-lb. carry-on, and a shoulder bag with wallet, money, cell phone, passport, and boarding pass.

Getting from Ananda's Gurgaon ashram at midnight, into a cab to the Delhi airport, and then to the airline counter—*without forgetting or losing an essential item*—became a major ordeal. Alas, though I am compulsively careful to assure that nothing is missing, something was missing when the cab was already in route, and we had to turn back. My phone had been left on a table where I'd set it while writing a note just before heading out the door.

I started to grouse about this bothersome twist, and then paused to think about where it fits in the longer rhythm of things. Essentially, it would soon disappear, having no effect whatsoever on the rest of my life.

What we really need to remember is to forget the voice inside us that causes us to lose our way back to God. Serving and supporting each other in a spirit of self-offering—in *self-forgetfulness*, that is—is what will speed our journey to Self-realization.

Among the great blessings we have before us is Swami Kriyananda's enormous creative output, achieved primarily by his self-forgetful attunement to his guru, Yogananda, and to God as Divine Mother. Nothing he ever did was about him. And nothing he ever accomplished was for personal gain. His sole motivation was to serve sincerely as their disciple, and by virtue of his humility and attunement, he was ever in bliss. As he wrote and sang in his song *In the Spirit*, "I was caught up in ecstasy. 'Twas a day sanctified by God. There He showed me the gifts of heaven, gifts that all seeking Him should know."

It is tempting to excuse ourselves from that level of consciousness, to say that Swamiji was simply more advanced than any of us. Maybe so. But wouldn't we all like to have what he had: inner peace and joy? Wouldn't we like to know what it means to be eternally free? Nobody gets there by asking, "What's in it for me?" Remembering to forget ourselves by giving the best that is in us is the key to the bliss we seek. Such is the yogi's way. Such is the way to claiming heaven's gifts right here on earth.

IT'S COMPLICATED.
OR ISN'T IT?

I've been thinking about the trap we set for ourselves in the judgments we make. The question of how much we like or dislike a person, object, feeling, experience, or idea, is certain to color how we react to every moment as it unfolds. The specific judgment can be as mundane as an attitude toward a new look in fashion, or as serious as the condition of one's health. The result is either pleasing or it isn't.

Westerners in particular tend to see in black or white: winners vs. losers, for instance. If you're not perceived as the former, you're apt to be branded the latter. Likewise, we obsess over good and bad, subconsciously guided to one label or the other, affixing it here and there automatically. As we see in disturbing abundance, simple issues of personal taste, not to mention morality, can quickly turn a dialogue into a feud. Different folks have different ideas about everything under the sun. Is it any wonder that complication prevails?

As a further complication, our certainties are not always certain. Think about how we think of war and peace. When we are not at war, are at peace? One might say yes, but hardly in absolute terms, because true peace is the absence of fear, and that describes almost no one. War and peace exist on the same wheel. As relative values, they show a direction of movement toward one or the other, not an unqualified state. The fabric of our lives is woven of both.

Love is another virtue that is often misrepresented. So much gets confused with emotion. It is said that every human act is either an expression of love or a cry for help. Where emotion runs deep, however, even a so-called act of love is tinged with insecurity as well. Emotional love is a transient. Born of desire, it conveys a form of attachment, which, by definition, involves the ego. Thus, the passion that emotional love ignites is bound to diminish. At its core, it is contractive. Surely we have all experienced how, as time goes by, complication tends to encumber even our most ardent relationships. Love of God is the one and only love that is ever expansive, for it alone is unaffected by circumstance or result. It alone is free of personal motive.

But is love of God a *practical* response to the whirl of our daily lives. Does it make sense to accept, without judgment, whatever comes down the pike? St.

Francis gave thanks for all that he received, no matter how meager or rude, as exactly what God had in mind for his spiritual growth. Was he just a good-hearted fool?

I doubt there is anything more difficult than letting go of one's emotional investments: that is to say, living without attachment to the outcome of our endeavors; learning to surrender our likes and dislikes to serve our soul. Yet, how else can we escape the sway of our fears? A popular mantra of the 1970s was "Give peace a chance." But what chance will it ever have if we, as mere reactionaries, continue to give a thumbs up or down to every person, item, and event that enters our field of awareness? This automatic exercise, harmless though it may seem, guarantees that fear of the unwanted will torment us. As duality ordains, every plus requires a canceling minus. Like night and day, every want must include its twin, whether in actual occurrence or the apprehension of same.

Of all the options we face, there is really but one that matters: either we roll our emotional investments into a more productive portfolio of stocks—compassion, forgiveness, introspection, meditation, and simple living, for example—or we keep falling short of the capital needed for inner peace, contentment, and unconditional love.

Could it be that faith in God is, after all, the most practical choice before us?

THE RISE OF INFORMANIA

As someone who remembers combing through dusty library stacks and pouring through pages of piled-high books for term-paper material, today's instant finger-touch access to every obscure fact under the sun is beyond astonishing. What Google and other search-engine wizards have accomplished is almost inconceivable. Now we have Wikipedia too, and countless other online resources for becoming conversant on every subject imaginable. Thanks to such innovation, however, we've become a world of incurable "informaniacs," certain that we are smarter than any culture has ever been.

But maybe not. A head full of information is not necessarily, and not even likely, an indication of knowing what needs to be known.

Information adds to the mind's encyclopedic storage. Although it takes up mental shelf-space, it can obviously be very useful and a boon to all. Having a lot of facts and figures at one's ready command on a range of topics also implies a higher intelligence and makes a good impression. This, for many reasons, would seem to be important.

Knowledge and wisdom, however, have more to do with subtraction than addition. They increase as the mind is emptied of mere information, making room for discernment and discrimination. Though the wise are seldom uninformed about worldly matters and essential "how to" approaches to problem-solving in general, they are also acutely aware of the limits that factual data are finally sure to reach. Because information offers no *experiential* component, it cannot provide the "extra mile" of understanding that is needed to grasp it fully.

Information maps the long way home, circumventing the heart and its arterial route to Spirit. Beware how much you take in.

CHAPTER 13

Poetry

"Poetry is indispensable – if I only knew what for!"

Jean Cocteau

LEAVING THE LOOP

Slowly, I am leaving the loop I have lived,
An expatriate in transition to another allegiance.
Dizzied by turns that return to the start,
And finding no reason but popular cause to continue,
I have inched my way to the edge of the track,
Fighting the urge of my feet to follow it 'round.
I can no longer circle uncertain of why,
Nor easily bring myself to break this looping habit.
I am in between,
But the die is cast.
From where I look now, the loop looks old and wearisome,
Its mystery yellow with age.
A kind of desolation contradicts its former lilt,
Played to the noisy tune of hurry and go.
Strange, the commitment to tedium's mode,
For little but folly leaps from its headlines now,
Much ado about what is ever the same.
The die is cast.
I am lighter now, beginning to leave the loop,
Closer to what comes next.

I Come to the Sea

I come to the sea to seek my soul
In the rolling-boil surf,
In the smooth glissade of the scouting tide,
In the whisper of spray and the chuckle of dispersing foam,
In the God of it all.

I come to the sea to release the one within me
Who knows of what I am,
To recollect and reconnect in rhyme;
Here in locomotive waves is the AUM,
Nine rows aroar at Cannon Beach;
Here is the One.

I come to the sea to breathe in mist and breeze
The forgotten life,
To memorize its renewal anew.

LESS AND LESS

Less and less do I care to own
That more and more will be mine;
Once unknown, freedom is grown
In modesty of design.

PARADOX

It's a paradox but true:
The more I make of me,
The less I am;
And the less I am,
The more I have to do.

A Song For the Road

Round and round
It goes as it goes,
Inside out
As root into rose.

Up and down
It goes as it goes,
End to end
Into endless flows.

> And it all goes diff'rent,
> And it all goes the same,
> Some goes better,
> Some goes to shame,
> And it all goes in order,
> And it all goes to ground,
> And it all goes as one goes
> As one goes around

On the road
In poem and prose,
Ever more
Are its highs and lows.

Once again,
As everyone knows,
Fast or slow,
It goes as it goes.

> And it all goes diff'rent,
> And it all goes the same,
> Some goes better,
> Some goes to shame,
> And it all goes in order,
> And it all goes to ground,
> And it all goes as one goes
> As one goes around.

THE DIFFERENCE

We think. But the mountain remembers.
We speak. But the river says more.
We compose. But never so well as the Muse.
We design. But who competes with spring?
We invent. But the heavens reveal.
We pretend. And none is our peer.

IN FLINT IS THE FIRE

In flint is the fire,
Awaiting the strike;
In seed is the sapling,
The universe,
All,
Awaiting the flood of rivers and tides
Held in a drop of rain;
In being is the evidence of love revealed,
Awaiting the veiled eye to see;
What more is there to know?
Mother, of Thee am I,
Awaiting the strike,
The fire and its light.

Into the Deep

Into the pause, do not hesitate,
Dive! Dive! Dive!
Between your thoughts, come alive!
Ever the masses, content to survive,
Miss the point, and do not arrive
Where the devotee enters the hive
And plunges deep.

I Could Not See What I Could Be

With eyes open, I am what I see;
With eyes closed, I am free.
I could not see what I could be
Until I could not see.

DISTRACTION

Distraction,

    my foe,

        my daily fare,

            I marvel at how you make up my mind.

To and from the stops on my agenda,

    you are,

        like a ticket to ride,

            my guide to the far and wide,

                my visa to the long way around.

How do I look?

    Was I noticed?

The Way It Seems To Be

Time to rest,
Find a nest,
For soon will come another test
. . . That suddenly is here!

No time to nest,
No time to rest,
For ever comes another test
. . . That suddenly is here!

DEADLINES

The ferry left at seven o'clock. Without him.
He remained in wishful sleep, in dream of being aboard,
In figment of crossing to higher self on the other side of the sea.
"Next time," he said, arising at eight. "Tomorrow I'll be there."

The ferry sailed without him again. And again.
For years of tomorrows it left before he arrived.
Deadlines held him ashore.
In time he called them his life.

On days he arose at six, his deadlines were waiting a five.
Two for every one he met, one for every two he set aside.
Promises to keep became his keeper, assigning him habits and tracks,
Keeping him kept.
Without him and without him the ferry withdrew.

Things remained as things remain,
Forming and deforming as he perceived.
He remained the same as well, only more so the more he achieved.
He willed himself a career and a house
And a lot of a lot he wanted along the way.
But never enough.
Enough was too little, then less.

On days he arose at five, his deadlines were waiting at four.
Seven would pass like a dream no longer remembered.
"A ferry is just a boat after all," he scribbled on a page in his head.
And so it sailed each day from within his reach,
Unreached.

As reason advised, he pressed ahead,
Revising his view to stay its revisionist course.
But as reason evolved, he struggled to hold his own.
Making sense began to make no sense. Could this be right?
What was he doing wrong?
What mattered if not the premise refined to a point?

Discouraged, he found himself courting despair,
Until, in despair, he found himself on his knees.
No miracle occurred.
But the lowering of his pride had a strangely uplifting effect.
Tethers, once tight, began to fray and release him.

Unable to understand this reversal of force,
He started to listen for clues between the cries of his conceit.
At last, in surrender, came a dispatch from inside him.
It bubbled like water, whispered like wind,
Echoing like the splendid silence at the bottom of a well.
Perhaps he was still asleep. Or losing his worldly mind.

As the sun slowly rose behind his eyes,
Colors began to appear on the gray walls within him,
Colors of melting allegiance to rules of thumb.
It was not yet six. He could make the ferry at seven.
Maybe this time he would.

To the Guru

O, poet, see my plight.
Lead me to your garden of verse, into your eternal day.
Introduce me to the fragrance of bliss,
The feel of blessed peace, the taste of communion.
Let me hear your voice in the flute,
Rising to blend with Lydian sounds of the harp,
Rising to meet the echoing of the bell,
Rising to play the wind.
New am I to the ways of intuition,
Old to the ways of reinventing the wheel.
Release me, loving one, from the tether of optical sight.
Baptize me in opalescent blue, redeem me in starry white.

O, poet, be the lotus of my lake,
Open your petals to me that I may see and understand,
Bathe my timid hope in God-romance.

DECEMBER

To all comes December,
Whether in winter or before,
And to all another birth,
In whereabouts unknown
Until it comes.

As my wife lay in bed, nearing the end of her life, and as I lay at her side…

SLIPPING AWAY

Slipping away,
She is slipping away,
Sadly, a little more each day,
Slipping, slipping away.

She struggles with uncertainty now,
Straining to be as she was,
Slipping into holding on,
Slipping slowly away.

So long, the we as we were,
So long, the once that used to be,
So odd, the unrescindable change,
So soon.

Slipping away,
She is slipping away,
Sadly, a little more each day,
So soon.

And then two weeks later…

When?

When?
When will it be?
Will it be when she says when?
When "Not yet" is no more?
Waiting for when is what we do
When its knowing is not yet now.

ARCHER, SEEK THE SHAFT OF LIGHT

Archer, seek the shaft of light
That lies within thy veiled sight,
And send it brightly at the night
That keeps thee bound in tension tight;
And let it lead thee into flight
That ferries darkness into might.

Archer, dare to bow the light
That offers thee a way from blight,
And send it at thy veiled sight
That keeps thee nightly bound to fright;
And let its course become thy plight
That plies thee to the ended fight.

Archer, choose to draw the light,
And send it into righted sight.

GET ALONG, LITTLE SELF, GET ALONE

Get along, little self, get alone.
Here is the where. Now is the when.
Go in, little self, go in.
Be gone. Be love in the morning.

On Writing

"Many people hear voices. Some are called mad and put into rooms where they sit and stare at the walls. Others are called writers, and they do pretty much the same thing."

Meg Chittenden

THE WAY WE ARE

"Sir, you've been staring out the window for the last thirty minutes," said the waitress to the man sitting at one of her tables. "You haven't moved a muscle except to sip your coffee. Are you ok?"

"Yes," he answered, without turning his head to meet her gaze.

"Is something on your mind?"

"Not yet," he replied, still staring ahead.

"What are you doing?"

"I'm working.

"Pardon me for asking, but what kind of work is staring and barely moving?"

"I'm a writer," he explained.

"Oh," she said, moving on.

⸺⸺⸺ ◦ ◈ ◦ ⸺⸺⸺

We who write are writing about ourselves, whether or not we're aware of it, no matter how we disguise it, whether we like it or not. We are at the core of the stories we tell, which change according to our angle of vision and the lighting we apply at the time, but only that. As the saying goes, the more things change, the more they stay the same.

I see myself and the world through the filter of my experience. As you read these essays, poems, and aphorisms, it is through your own filter that you will decide if what is written rings true, and if it inspires you or turns you off. From here on, I have no ability to affect your response.

Mordecai Richler once declared that all writing is essentially about dying, "about the brief flicker of time we have here, and the frustrations it creates." Maybe so, but I like to think that my own writing is less about the frustrations and more about how to undo them. That is what I hope my story is now, and that you find it useful to that end also.

It is the writer's nature to wish that what he has written might have been written better. And so he revisits, revises, and revises again, until he happily strikes the note he was seeking or simply wearies of the battle, allowing his final version, whether a mere sentence or a book, to represent the measure of his skill. In coming upon a piece in later years, he will sometimes find himself pleasantly surprised at how well it reads, but often he will be reminded that he should have revised it again.

As a writer, I serve at the wonder and whim of what happens in my life, especially of what happens to me. These events inform my writing and take it where they want it to go. I am merely along for the ride, hopefully paying attention and keeping track.

Language cannot reveal or express the depth or fullness of life. It arrives on the scene after the doing is done. Although it may embellish what has occurred, it remains a generation removed. Language is to experience as rumor is to truth. Even when it is right, it is just a reporter.

No matter the medium, from literature to landscape painting to landscaping itself, there is perhaps no greater artistic challenge than deciding what to leave out. Anyone can include too much, and such is the common mistake that condemns a work to its ultimate mediocrity, even when finely rendered.

If you would be a writer of works intended for others to read, give them writing that invites them to explore your subject as if it were theirs.

For balance, inspiration, and inner renewal, I often find that I need to get lost. This can be done even in a crowd. Mostly, though, I prefer to slip away, into the quiet of my room, or wander alone in nature in the society of trees and sky. Mental adventure does not require a physical component, only the will to duck inside yourself and break down a fence or two.

Sometimes a friend will join me on these solitary excursions, lending conversation and insight to my escape. As I have found over the years, it is frequently easier to enjoy another's company when there's no actual person there to add complexity to the exchange.

Every person's story has a sacred dimension. Yet, too many writers give it little or no attention. In this partly dysfunctional and often dangerous world, the need for us to write more enlightened stories is critical to our shared global well-being.

I could not have planned this book. Even when I had ideas about what it would be, page after page was presented to me in surprise. Writing, no less than reading, you see, is done to discover what awaits to be said.

Shakespeare, Whitman and Dickinson are dead, but thank God we have their poetry to remind us what poetry is. Today, to a great extent, the word has been arrogated to describe a form of writing that is more like a body of hastily scribbled messages in coded language. Loneliness, angry spatter, and a lack of talent are often the only substance that is conveyed. The popular "poetry slam" is mostly a staging for the arcane to appear creative, which tends to prove only the opposite. Obfuscation is the common device of today's would-be poet, aided and abetted by insensitivity, a-lyrical meter and long-winded incoherence. Bless you, Billy Collins and a few others, for keeping the medium alive.

Can we please find another word for "blog" ?!?!!! It sounds like something you should do before leaving the house and never in public. As a reference to a popular writing form, "blog" is about as anti-literate and uninspiring as a word could be. I cannot imagine a respected journalist wanting to be known as a "blogger." The title is better suited to someone convicted of assault and battery, which is also what many blogs are guilty of committing.

I wish to nominate the re-use of "columnist" or "essayist" for any such person who is serious about writing well, and is schooled in the refinements of grammar and interesting content. I know this is the Computer Age, replete with abbreviated phrases and descriptions, but let's not cast all sense of language and style into coarse convenience.

I have called myself a writer. Whether or not others would say that I am, I cannot say. But of this I am certain: It is I who belong to what I have written, not the writing to me.

Chapter 15

Essays in a Sentence or Two

"One cannot collect all the beautiful shells on the beach.
One can collect only a few, and they are
more beautiful if they are a few."

Anne Morrow Lindbergh

One who speaks unkindly should not expect to be understood.

If you want it, be the first to give it away: love, loyalty, appreciation, support, or just a smile.

Truth is all that really counts. It is at our peril that we ignore or distort it, for it alone will have the final say.

A good idea that originates in a fool is still a good idea, and a poor one raised by a genius is poor nonetheless. Weigh the idea for its worth, regardless of its source.

A compromise can be crafted that upholds the integrity of principle, but a principle cannot be compromised with integrity.

Reach out lovingly to others. The need is great for many people to know that someone cares. Be a light in their lives, if only for the moment of passing through.

Adhere to truth, and you have won, despite what others may say. Succumb to a compromise of it, and you have lost the purpose of why you are here, despite what others may say.

There's a nasty sort of pleasure in finding fault in others. But in self-congratulation, the nastiness remains when the pleasure has gone.

Observe yourself as if from above. Too often we lose perspective by engaging at ground zero in the canyons of our problems and pursuits. There is more to see, and more to be, from higher up.

If someone upsets you, what do *you* need to work on?

Modern life is awash in complication. It undermines our relationships, our work, and even our play. Simplify how you think, and think smarter. Simplify what you have, and have more. Simplify how you live, and live better. Simplify!

The way to do what you cannot do is to start learning how to do it by starting to do it.

If you stand where you are, you will not stub your toe. Nor will you get ahead, which will hurt a lot more.

The trouble with a status quo is that people develop a stake in its duration, which they tend to defend beyond the time its quo has run out of status.

When hubris takes the helm, the heart is overruled for no good reason.

You may be a student of exceptional acuity and analytical skill, but until you have lived whatever it is you have studied, you do not know it.

Nature abhors a vacuum, but in view of what we have often used to fill the ones that occur, a vacuum would have been preferable.

To guarantee the persistence of a long-term problem, apply short-term thinking… as most governments, corporations, and stressed out people do.

The best part of getting rid of desires is getting rid of the work required to entertain and pursue them.

Mighty though the massive oak, it is no match for the tiny microbe that will, at last, quietly and unseen, reduce it to soil.

Some would say the opposite of reason is madness, and yet madness has often been the result of what we reason to do.

We pray to be free of temptation. But only after temptation has taken us down. And only for a short time after that.

If it worries you, it owns you.

The problem part of most problems is our problem-minded approach to getting rid of it.

We cannot unlive the past, but we can remake it by living differently now.

———————

Death is the musical drone in the opus of life, the underscore that is always there. No life would be as full without its note.

———————

One is never more at risk than when he is overly cautious.

———————

We plan to live, but not to die,
      And so we live for that which passes by,
      And die unprepared.

———————

The trouble is, we believe we need higher technology to eliminate disease, stress, insecurity, and the like, the primary cause of which is the growth of higher technology.

———————

If you would reach the graveyard sooner than later, follow the ruts.

———————

The problem in learning patience is the patience it takes to learn it.

———————

Someone here is annoying me. I wonder if it could be me!

The trouble is, the Escape key on my computer doesn't work. I'm still here.

The answer to "Are we there yet?" is always yes. It's just that "there" is not where most of us probably had in mind.

If you wish to be understood, watch carefully what you say, for words are slippery things, and the mind can be rather clumsy at catching their drift.

The beauty and wonder we find in travel is only as much as the beauty and wonder we have carried with us. Attunement and receptivity are the keys to every experience, and they are not tools of the external world. The journey is always made from within.

God said "Give," and we heard "Get," and what we have been getting ever since is the karma that is given for faulty hearing and stubborn adherence to it.

If you would be here now, you must take off your "expectacles" and own the moment as it is.

... And remember: You must be present to win.

A Few More Personals: Then and Now

"Grow old along with me,

The best is yet to be,

The last of life, for which the first was made. . ."

Robert Browning

I was born and raised a Catholic. Throughout my formative years, the Church instilled its catechism in me, and by the time I passed through puberty, confusion, conflict, and guilt were among my regular companions.

Thanks to my parents, my formal education was among the best that anyone could hope for. Beverly Hills High School and Stanford University were exceptional schools that saw to my intellectual grooming and well-rounded socialization. As I entered adulthood, I appeared to be on the cusp of a finely prepared, conventional rest of my life. I was a "nice young man," seldom a problem for anyone, with my ego firmly, but not conceitedly, at the helm of who I had become.

In the more than fifty years since then, much has changed in me, and many times over. The Catholic Church has long since disappeared from my rearview mirror, replaced by a spirituality that I trust as truer than any institutional system for ascending to salvation. Along the way, my conventional life has taken numerous unconventional turns; and yet I am still a pragmatist, still rather intellectual, and still contending with the exhortations of my ego.

I left the Church when I was twenty years old, although some of it had leached into my bones. It troubled me for decades, in particular its hellish reminders of the cost I incurred for every mortal, testosterone-driven sin I committed. For a while I flirted with atheism, mostly because it appealed to my '60s, anti-establishment leanings at the time. Then, a few years later, a friend took me to a lecture in Ojai, California, by J. Krishnamurti. His message and manner were riveting to me, especially his profound vision of what is real and what is not. I started to read his books, and I went to see him again in Santa Monica. That was my introduction to Eastern philosophy. It attracted me in a way that Western religious doctrine never had.

The magical possibilities in the books of Carlos Castaneda made a second important impression on me. This was a "heady" time, and I did not decline the altered-state opportunities that were offered to me. The trips I took were mostly sincere journeys of self-discovery, which opened my mind to a dazzling new dimension of possibilities. In breaking away from the only knowns I had known, I began to see that I had more to explore and expose than before.

I studied the *Tao Te Ching*, and later *The Tao of Physics* by Fritjof Capra. The science of quantum theory and its spiritual implications were thrilling to me, and are even more so today. There's a third Tao on my bookshelf too: *The Tao of Pooh* by Benjamin Hoff. If you haven't read it, it's a delightful gem of gentle wisdom.

There is no need here to go into depth about *Autobiography of a Yogi*, which set me squarely on the spiritual path to Self-realization that I have been on since 1996. The principles, truths, and teachings contained within it are woven through much of this book of mine. So is the content of Swami Kriyananda's mere 150 books and countless lectures. To a great extent I have simply put into words and images of my own what they have written before me.

I grew up playing baseball. It was "America's pastime," and it was my favorite way to pass time too. I still say it's the greatest team game ever invented—brilliantly mental as well as artfully physical when played well—with more subtleties of strategy than any of the faster and more aggressive games that may have a larger fan base today.

My parents wanted me to learn the piano. I took lessons and practiced, but not with dedication. I wanted to be outside playing ball in the street, in the park, and on our school's playground. I was good at the game, and "totally into it." So were my closest friends. The piano didn't last—and I'm sorry for that, because I love music, and would love to be able to sit at the keyboard and soothe my soul with a repertoire of favorite pieces—but baseball won my heart. My only regret for the game is that it is played too often now by professional athletes who love it less for the joy of the sport than the obscene salaries they are allowed to receive.

I played baseball through high school, got into Stanford in part because of my prowess, but did not even make the freshman team, a casualty of the curveball, which I had never hit consistently well. Now those breakers were really breaking sharply. I retired from the sport at age 19.

These days the game that has my attention is called "Get Me to God," in which I am yet a minor-leaguer trying to make it to the majors. Like the many who labor throughout their careers, fated to take the field year after year with the Tennessee Smokies or Sacramento River Cats instead of the Dodgers or Yankees, those of us who struggle to measure up in a spiritual sense may yet be lifetimes away from Divine reunion. We persevere, but the call does not come that would free us from our limitations. Maybe one's "curveball" is a restless mind; or, like a weak throwing arm, an underdeveloped feeling of devotion. A player may be skilled, but not necessarily skilled enough to be among the elite, the sainted few.

In baseball and on the spiritual path, what matters most, however, is love of what you are doing. We make errors in the field, we strike out with runners in scoring position, we get tagged out trying to steal a base. But if we are here for love of the game, doing our best to round the bases for home, Spirit applauds.

The guys in the majors have their bad days too. They lose their concentration, letting opportunities die. They hit into rally-ending double plays. Who doesn't know about that? But every time at bat is a chance to score, and for those who are in it for love, it is always the majors.

It is fascinating to observe how we age. The mind, persistently in denial, continues to think of itself in the prime of youth, even as its acuity slips increasingly below its youthful performance. We remember how fast we could run, how agile we were, how long we could last in a test of endurance, and we don't quite get the disconnect between memory and today's reality. Meanwhile, the flesh wrinkles and cracks, joints creak and ache, physical strength weakens, and stamina wanes. It's a humbling experience that for many induces frustration and resentment.

I am one of the lucky ones, and I am sincerely grateful for the health and vigor I have been blessed to maintain. Few who are my age have been so fortunate. But for over twenty years now, people have called me mister and sir, failing to see me as I see myself. In India I am "uncle" to kids and strangers who would call me "cousin" if I were not viewed as much older. And when younger women flirt with me today, they are no longer serious about it. Ouch!

It's not that I am unused to these titles and gestures of respect, or that I do not appreciate them. But I miss being mistaken for a man who is not of my vintage. Like iodine on an open cut, the politeness stings a little.

Yet, I have memories of an era that younger generations will never know as richly as I who lived them. I grew up in a special time and place, in years that were simpler and sweeter than any I have known since. There is treasure in that, and I would not trade it for the attributes that I can no longer claim. It is more than just nostalgia, it is melody and joy.

My boyhood was a time of radio and trains, and my imagination ran with the vivid scenes that both of these conjured up for me. Before we got our first TV in 1950, radio was my ticket to comedy and adventure. Seated in our living room in front our big Philco, and in the family Buick well into the '50s, we listened with rapt attention to *Amos 'n Andy, Jack Benny, the Lone Ranger, Red Ryder, Fibber McGee 'n Molly, The Shadow,* and other popular weekly shows.

I also remember sitting with Mom in 1949 when word came out of the box that war had broken out in Korea, and that America would be involved. I was six years old, and had no idea what that could mean, but Mom was deeply troubled. It meant that Dad might be called back into the Army. Thankfully, he wasn't, but I can still see the look on her face.

As much as I also loved all the programs on early TV, there was something extra special about the radio. Years later, commentator Alistair Cooke asked a classroom of children which they preferred, radio or TV. Only one of them raised his hand in favor of radio. "Why?" Cooke asked. "I like the pictures better," said the boy. When I thought about it, that would have been my answer too. Radio theater is about the "audio visuals' that dance in your head.

As a young adult, I wrote and directed dozens of radio commercials for Disney and other clients, always trying to weave a little storyline delight into the pitch. I had the pleasure during those years to work sometimes with Ray Ehrlenborn, a sound effects wizard from the old days of live radio broadcasting. Ray had a large, vaudeville-style suitcase of props for just about every sound you could want to produce, and what he didn't have in the suitcase he could do with his mouth. God, it was fun to work with him.

Trains were like magic carpets for me too: Pullman sleeper cars and scenic dome cars especially. At a young age, I traveled overland a couple of times on the Super Chief from Chicago to LA or the other way back, and I can still see many of the glorious scenes of the West as we rolled through them. Visions of cowboys and Indians danced in my head, and when we rode through buffalo country, or pulled into Albuquerque, there they were on horseback or meeting the train in full regalia for a photo op. I was with my heroes.

The sound of train wheels on the track are hypnotizing too. It's like a mystical monologue that sweeps you into the heart of it, even though you don't know the language, recounting stories of a pioneering past. And climbing into the top bunk of a Pullman car, lulled to sleep by the sound of those wheels and gentle jerkiness of the train's vibration. . . well, it doesn't get any better than that for a kid in love with adventure.

In 1990 my wife and I rode the rails in Europe on a four-month pass. We could hop on a train whenever we wanted, and that's what we did: along the Rhine, through the Alps, into splendid forests and across majestic plains. If our funds had been without limit, we might be there still, riding from one discovery to another. The romance of traveling on trains never seems to get old.

But life is different for those who are young today. Technology has brought the world's mysteries and wonders to our laptops and phones, and literally to our fingertips. In my wildest dreams as a youth, I could not have imagined how far we have come in connectivity to information and, superficially, to each other.

Yet, these achievements have also come at a cost. I believe that our spirit of adventure and imagination has suffered a serious loss. The half-life of innocence is half of what it once was. Magic is taken for granted at the price of its charm, and virtual reality is deterring us from exploring and experiencing the real thing. We are smarter in certain ways perhaps, but the total effect is both dumbing and dulling us down.

Young people today will have their fond memories too as they get older, but I do not envy the quality of what those memories are likely to be. For those getting back to the land, however, back to simplicity and the heart of being, mystery and wonder will continue to be their teachers, and it is they I will seek as mentors when I return again. They will have the next equivalent of radio and trains to stir a child's creative imagination.

People see me as disciplined, and in some ways I am. But I am also acutely aware of propensities in me that belie that image. They are why I am still here as a human being, and why I probably will be again, toiling to reach enlightenment and God-reunion.

I am not one, however, to seek the easy way out, because I know it does not exist. Since I was a kid, I have taken risks that I reckoned would serve me well, even if I did not succeed in gaining the goal that was sought. The real goal was acting on the risk itself, for in that comes the growth that leads to more of the same.

Many of the risks I took back then were in the arena of sports. I was a good athlete, and I pushed myself to improve the skills I developed. The most daring of the challenges I gave myself was getting into the boxing ring at Stanford. During the year I fought on the varsity team, I was never without trepidation when stepping in against my opponent, especially when an audience was there. Thankfully, I performed well, but maybe I would have learned more if my ego had been dealt a knock-down or embarrassing loss.

Yet, it's funny how often I pardon myself for failing to push through resistances that would seem much easier and safer to overcome. My spiritual practices often play second fiddle to pursuits of evanescent pleasures that are merely escapist. Although far less noble and brave, I share a flaw with Karna, the great warrior of the Bhagavad Gita, who believed that lasting happiness could be found in the world around him. My love of this earth and its beauties, of friends and time together, and even of activities that serve no inner purpose, tends to preempt me from choosing austerities that would better serve my soul. Consequently, my meditations are frequently shorter and drier than a yogi should accept without exercising more discipline.

My ability to focus at length is primarily as a writer. The process is not merely intellectual, for the heart must be engaged where sensitivity and attunement are essential to "getting it right." But I also use writing as an excuse for neglecting longer meditations and other transcendent practices. I envy those who love to meditate more than anything else. I wish I were one of them, but still I am not.

———◦—◦—◦———

From a dream I once had about twenty years ago, generously embellished…

As I stood before the Gatekeeper, he asked me, "What did you do with your life?

"Advertising and sales," I proudly replied.

"I see," he said with a furrowed brow, "you encouraged others to buy what they did not need so that you could do the same."

"Whoa," I objected, "that's a bit heavy on the downside, don't you think?"

"I just call 'em as I see 'em," he said making notes.

"I did the best I could for every client," I tried to assure him. "Every campaign got my full creative attention and support. I even won some awards."

"Awards for what?" he asked without really asking. "For helping to perpetuate people's desires, delusions, and greed? For persuading your neighbors that whatever you were selling, they'd be unhappy without it?"

"Or happier with it," I quickly rebutted. "I favored a positive outlook. And I was helping to make the economy strong. That is what I was taught."

"That is what you chose to learn," he corrected. "You chose to be as the many instead of the few. You sought worldly success instead of your soul's freedom."

"Do I get another chance?" I pleaded. "Can I go back and give it another try?"

"Oh, yes," he nodded with a wry smile, "we quite insist that you do!"

———◦—◦—◦———

My heroes have been many, most of them highly skilled in some field of human endeavor, all of them humble, courageous, generous, and kind. I have written of Shihan, my karate instructor, and extensively of Swami Kriyananda. People who do what they do for the love of the doing are the ones who have my undivided attention and admiration, no matter how modest the doing may be.

Living in Beverly Hills throughout the '50s and early '60s, during grade school and high school, I met many of the rich and famous, some of whom were folks just like the rest of us, and many whose ambitions were greater than their better qualities. The latter were often the ones who were most insecure, more driven by their sense of image than happy with the result. I did not envy them even then.

In the late '60s, when I was starting out in the advertising business, I worked for a large agency in Los Angeles that had a number of major accounts. One of these was Richfield Oil, which later merged with Atlantic Oil, to form ARCO, a giant of the industry ever since. Richfield was a TV sponsor of UCLA basketball and its coach's weekly show on KTLA. I was the client's producer on that show, which amounted to little of importance, but it meant that I was present for each of the live telecasts. And I wouldn't have missed them for anything, because that coach and those teams were the greatest that college basketball has ever seen.

Coach John Wooden, the "Wizard of Westwood," was one of the finest human beings to walk this planet. His teams won ten national championships, a feat that will surely never be matched by anyone. But coach Wooden was in the business of building boys into men of character, and to play for him meant putting your personal growth—spiritual growth, really—ahead of even basketball. His work ethic was demanding; self-discipline and faith were the values he instilled in his players; and his ways were as caring and kind as they were strict.

Lew Alcindor, later known as Kareem Abdul Jabbar, one of the greatest college and NBA players of all time, was among the young men that coach Wooden molded into more than a stellar athlete. And I got to rub elbows with him, the coach, and dozens of others every week. I was in heaven.

Coach Wooden proved a point that is still overlooked by the vast majority of coaches and athletes in almost every sporting field and in life itself: that winning starts with developing more than talent; that when you focus first on developing the inner person, winning takes care of itself, because no one who is centered in the strength of his deeper self is ever a loser.

My life has been blessed over and over by those such as John Wooden, who have been a part of my time on this precious earth. Within Ananda are many score more just like him, men and women who are saints in the making, dedicated to helping others reach their highest potential by cultivating the soul's nature within them. If there is a better way to live, I cannot imagine what it would be.

About the Author

Surendra James Conti is an essayist, teacher, world traveler, and avid observer of the human scene. A man of many interests and careers, his resume includes: copywriter and broadcast producer for Walt Disney Productions; fine art dealer of Old Master prints; manager of America's premier metaphysical bookstore, East West Bookshop, in Mountain View, California; ordained minister of the Ananda Church of Self-Realization; and spiritual director of Ananda's yoga ashram in Pune, India. He is currently the director of Ananda Portland's Temple and Teaching Center in Oregon. His spiritual name, Surendra, was given to him by Swami Kriyananda. Its Sanskrit meaning is "he who offers himself in service to God."